THE MUSIC OF LORD BERNERS (1883–1950)

For my parents

The Music of Lord Berners (1883–1950)

'The Versatile Peer'

BRYONY JONES

ASHGATE

Published by
Ashgate Publishing Limited
Gower House
Croft Road
Aldershot
Hampshire GU11 3HR
England

Ashgate Publishing Company
Suite 420
101 Cherry Street
Burlington, VT 05401-4405 USA

Ashgate website: http://www.ashgate.com

British Library Cataloguing in Publication Data
Jones, Bryony
    The music of Lord Berners (1883–1950) : 'the versatile peer'
    1. Berners, Gerald Hugh Tyrwhitt-Wilson, Baron, 1883–1950 -
    Contributions in music 2. Music - Great Britain - 20th
    century - History and criticism
    I. Title
    780.9'2

Library of Congress Cataloging-in-Publication Data
Jones, Bryony.
    The music of Lord Berners (1883–1950) : the versatile peer / Bryony Jones.
        p. cm.
    Includes bibliographical references, discography, and index.
    ISBN 0-7546-0852-2 (alk. paper)
        1. Berners, Gerald Hugh Tyrwhitt-Wilson , Baron, 1883–1950--Criticism and
interpretation. I. Title.

MT92.B46 J6 2002
780'.92--dc21
[B]   2002066591

ISBN 0 7546 0852 2

Printed and bound in Great Britain by MPG Books Ltd, Bodmin, Cornwall

Contents

Preface

19 April 2000 marked the fiftieth anniversary of the death of Gerald Tyrwhitt-Wilson, 14th Baron Berners, and during the week 17–21 April he was BBC Radio 3's 'Composer of the Week'. A revival of interest in Berners' music in evidence around the centenary of his birth seemed to have fizzled out by the late 1980s, but emerged again in the mid 1990s, and a number of new recordings of his works – including some which had never before been released – date from that time. These recordings, mostly issued on the Marco Polo label, have played an important role in my research. Most of the published scores are easily available through inter-library loans, but to have been able to hear the works performed has been a tremendous advantage.

The majority of Berners' manuscripts are now held at the British Library, and the completion of my list of works (Appendix 2) would have been impossible without access to these. Fortunately, too, Berners wrote his scores in a meticulously neat hand!

Chapter 1: Berners' Character and Career is not intended as an extensive biographical study, but rather as an introduction to Berners' life; readers who wish to know more about Berners' character are directed to Mark Amory's biography *Lord Berners The Last Eccentric* (Chatto and Windus, 1998). The aim of *my* book is to examine Berners' music, to investigate who influenced his style, and to follow the progression from small-scale pieces he wrote early in his career to the large-scale ballets which brought him to wider public attention later on. Chapters 2–6 are broadly arranged in chronological order, although some overlaps were unavoidable. The final chapter examines why Berners was forgotten so soon after his death, and follows the development of new interests in his work.

All the extracts from Berners' music are reproduced by permission of Chester Music.

Bryony Jones

Acknowledgements

I should like to express my gratitude to Professor Robert Orledge at the University of Liverpool for his supportive guidance and friendly advice over my three years of work on Lord Berners, and to Professor Michael Talbot without whose encouragement my original Masters dissertation would not have grown into this book. I cannot express highly enough my appreciation for the helpful and encouraging atmosphere which prevails in the Music Department of the University of Liverpool. I should like to acknowledge, too, the value of the Henry Watson Music Library in Manchester as an important resource for researchers in the North West of England. Peter Dickinson's editorial notes in the Chester publications of Berners' collected piano and vocal music were an invaluable aid when completing the list of works in Appendix 2; Mark Amory's 1998 biography of Berners has been a wealth of information. Finally, I must thank my parents: my mother for the many hours spent trawling through microfilm with me in Manchester's Central Library in the hope of finding a few needles in a very large haystack, and for proof-reading everything that I put in front of her; my father for use of his large record collection; and both of them for their constant support and encouragement.

Chapter 1

Berners' Character and Career

Gerald Tyrwhitt, later the 14th Lord Berners,[1] was born at Apley Park, Shropshire, on 18 September 1883. He was the only son of naval Captain Hugh Tyrwhitt (third son of Emma Harriet, Baroness Berners in her own right)[2] and Julia Mary Foster, the daughter of an extremely wealthy local businessman. Gerald was initially educated at home by a private tutor, but was sent to boarding school at the age of nine, first to Cheam, then, four years later in 1897, to Eton. At this stage of his life it was by no means certain that Gerald would inherit the barony; he had an unmarried uncle, Raymond Tyrwhitt,[3] to whom it would pass first, and if the uncle were to marry and have children the title would automatically pass to them after his death. If Raymond Tyrwhitt were to die without having children, the Berners title would then pass to Gerald's father, and only after *his* death would Gerald inherit. Even if it looked possible that Gerald would eventually succeed to the title, there was no way of knowing when it might happen. On completion of his studies at Eton, therefore, it was considered necessary for him to find a suitable career; the diplomatic corps was suggested by his mother,[4] and at the age of sixteen he was sent to Normandy, then Dresden, Vienna and Italy to learn languages as preparation for this vocation. Despite never actually passing his diplomacy examinations he achieved a post as honorary attaché to the British

---

[1] Gerald has occasionally been referred to as the 9th Baron. Obituaries in *The Times* incorrectly named his grandmother's uncle the 6th Baron and his uncle, Raymond Tyrwhitt, the 8th (they were actually the 11th and 13th). By the time Gerald's obituary was written, the mistake had been corrected and he was properly referred to as the 14th Baron. However, seven months later, when the same paper reported the details of his will, he was referred to as the 9th Baron, and a few other sources have since copied the mistake. Even discounting the three baronesses in the Berners line, the numbers do not add up. Debrett's Peerage names the entire line, and Gerald is quite clearly the 14th Baron Berners.

[2] The Berners barony is one of the few which can be passed down through the female as well as male line.

[3] Baroness Berners' eldest son, Harry Tyrwhitt Wilson (1855–1891) died before his mother, two days after his 36th birthday.

[4] Amory states that it was Gerald's father who suggested diplomacy as a career (Amory, 1998, 27) but in the second volume of his autobiography *A Distant Prospect* (1945, reprinted 1998, 169) Berners implies that it was his mother's idea.

embassies in Constantinople in 1909, and Rome in 1911.[5] The work was far from taxing but during this time Gerald developed a love of Europe which would remain with him throughout his life. A strong interest in music, which had not been encouraged by his family when at home, also began to flourish now he was beyond their jurisdiction, and he started to compose seriously, having his first published works, *Trois petites marches funèbres*,[6] published in Italy under the name Gerald Tyrwhitt before he became Lord Berners.

Hugh Tyrwhitt had died suddenly in October 1907 while on board the steamship 'Caledonia' en route to Port Said from Marseilles and had been buried at sea. His mother, Lady Berners, died ten years later in 1917 and her second son Raymond, the 13th Lord Berners, died the following year at the age of 63. He had remained unmarried and childless so in 1918 Gerald succeeded to the title of Berners[7] and returned to England to claim his inheritance. The speed of events had taken him somewhat by surprise and he remained working at the embassy in Rome until June 1919. Encouraged by the opinions of Stravinsky and the Italian composer, pianist and conductor Alfredo Casella,[8] who had seen some of his early piano music, he then relinquished his career and returned to England determined to devote more time to composition. The inheritance enabled him to spend the rest of his life in relative luxury, dividing his time between England, France, Italy and Germany, and occupying himself by socialising, composing, writing novels and painting without the ties of a career in the embassy; a well-known figure, he gained the title 'the versatile peer' in the national press.

Berners' talents in music, literature and painting earned him respect from many of the great artistic minds of the day. Though his musical output was relatively small it drew high praise from Stravinsky; one of his works was even performed alongside *The Rite of Spring* in its English premiere.

---

[5] According to Amory, Gerald was appointed in September 1911 but only arrived in December (Amory, 1998, 48).

[6] The *Trois petites marches funèbres* were Berners first published works but not his first mature compositions. See Appendix 2 for more information.

[7] On the death of his uncle, Gerald became both the 14th Lord Berners *and* a baronet (a title which had been passed down through his paternal grandfather's line). He also became Tyrwhitt-Wilson by royal licence in 1919: Wilson was the maiden name of Berners' grandmother, Lady Berners, and by tradition her heirs had added this to their names.

[8] 1883–1947. Casella used a passage from Berners' 'Pour une tante à l'héritage' from *Trois petites marches funèbres* in his book *The Evolution of Music throughout the history of the Perfect Cadence* (London, J & W Chester Ltd, 1924).

He wrote for Diaghilev's Ballets Russes, met Berg and Schoenberg in Salzburg, had works conducted by Sir Thomas Beecham, Eugene Goossens, Ernest Ansermet and Constant Lambert, and collaborated on musical projects with Sacheverell Sitwell, Gertrude Stein, Penelope Betjeman and Frederick Ashton. He published numerous piano pieces and songs in English, French and German. His ballets were staged in London, Monte Carlo and New York, and he had an opera performed in Paris in 1924. He also completed two film scores for Ealing Studios in the 1940s.

In addition to his achievements as a composer, Berners published six novels and two volumes of autobiography (a third, which was unfinished at the time of his death, was published in 2000 under the title *The Château de Résenlieu*). Two exhibitions of his paintings, held in London in May 1931 and July 1936, sold out, and he wrote a play, *The Furies*, which ran for one week at the Oxford Playhouse in 1942. Walton dedicated *Belshazzar's Feast* to him, and such celebrities as Aldous Huxley, Wallis Simpson, Salvador Dali, John Betjeman and Rex Whistler[9] visited his various homes. In 1935 he built the last traditional folly tower in England[10] at his home in Faringdon, Berkshire. Today the octagonal tower still looms large over the surrounding countryside, standing one hundred feet tall, and is open to the public on the first Sunday of every month. The tower was designed and constructed by the architect Gerald Wellesley,[11] but an argument between him and Berners resulted in its being built mostly in a classical style but with a Gothic top ten feet.

Unfortunately in the years following his death in 1950, Berners came to be remembered, if at all, as little more than an eccentric aristocrat who dyed his pigeons various pastel shades and who entertained Penelope Betjeman's horse to tea in one of his country homes. However, among his contemporaries he was seen not only as a remarkably talented man but also as one of the great wits of his generation. Tremendously faithful to his friends, Berners enjoyed immense popularity among those who knew him best. Diana Mosley summed up the comments of many others when she described him in *Loved Ones, Pen Portraits*: 'Clever, talented, witty,

---

[9] Rex Whistler (1905–44) completed a portrait of Berners in 1929. It is on display at the National Portrait Gallery, London.
[10] In 1936 Berners painted an advertising poster for Shell which showed the Faringdon Folly with the caption 'To visit Britain's Landmarks you can be sure of Shell'. A copy of this poster, along with other examples of Berners' artwork, can be seen in Mark Steyn's article 'Lord Berners as a Painter', *Apollo*, August 1984.
[11] Wellesley became the seventh Duke of Wellington in 1943.

original and private-spirited, he was the best companion as well as the most loyal friend anyone could be lucky enough to have.'[12]

Berners was undoubtedly multi-talented, but he was also a complex character whose fondness for humour – especially playing practical jokes on both friends and enemies – was often at odds with the feelings of depression and inadequacy that dogged him throughout his life. He is described by Osbert Sitwell in *Laughter in the Next Room*, the second of his four volumes of autobiography, as follows:

> Melancholy I believe by nature, and with a number of talents of uncommon degree most evenly distributed among the arts, when not at work he is addicted to wit or humour as less gifted individuals are victims to drink or drugs. It is difficult to drag him away from a joke, and he would willingly return to it.[13]

Described as 'an unabashed hedonist',[14] Berners found humour and enjoyment the best way to avoid sinking into a depressive state and he worked hard to keep it that way. In later life he tended to use his eccentricity specifically to entertain others, so that which had been initially spontaneous became cultured, though its effect never seems to have dulled. Berners was the inspiration behind the character Lord Merlin in Nancy Mitford's semi-autobiographical novel *The Pursuit of Love* (1945), and he later parodied himself as Lord FitzCricket in his short novel *Far From the Madding War* (1941). There is no doubting the identity of FitzCricket, and Berners' description is written with characteristic modesty:

> He was always referred to by gossip-column writers as "the versatile peer," and indeed there was hardly a branch of art in which he had not at one time or other dabbled. He composed music, he wrote books, he painted; he did a great many things with a certain facile talent. He was astute enough to realise that, in Anglo-Saxon countries, art is more highly appreciated if accompanied by a certain measure of eccentric publicity. This fitted in well with his natural inclinations.[15]

While at Eton, Berners was never as popular among his peers as he was to become later in life. However, a comment in *A Distant Prospect*, the second volume of his autobiography, describes how his musical talents

---

[12] 1985, 131.
[13] 1950, 177.
[14] Acton, 1984, xi.
[15] 1941, 127–28.

earned him unexpected esteem from several of his older and more distinguished schoolmates. It reveals how he discovered that music could be used to please others:

> How fortunate it was…that my musical taste had a more frivolous side that could be exploited to entertain the great.[16]

Berners was far more interested in exercising his wit and carrying out practical jokes than he was in the more serious matters of the time. Politics held no interest for him whatsoever, 'he went only once to the House of Lords and refused to go again because a bishop stole his hat'.[17] His love of humour often found expression in nonsense verse. One example, comes from his time working at the embassy in Constantinople:

> A thing that Uncle George detests
> Is finding mouse shit in his vests
> But what he even more abhors
> Is seeing Auntie in her drawers.[18]

Another is quoted by Harold Acton, and refers to a Salvador Dali picture bought by Berners when he became interested in Surrealism:

> On the pale yellow sands
> There's a pair of clasped Hands
> And an Eyeball entangled with string…
> And a Bicycle Seat
> And a Plate of Raw Meat
> And a Thing that is hardly a Thing.[19]

He loved to offer people misleading information; on one occasion he invited a particularly eager social climber to dinner with the promise that the 'P of W' would also be attending. Hastily charging off to dine with the Prince of Wales, she was greeted instead by Berners and the Provost of Worcester![20] In *First Childhood*, the first volume of his autobiography, Berners frequently volunteers such deceptive information. Names of people

---

[16] 1945, 2nd ed. 1998, 53.
[17] Steyn, 1983, 32.
[18] Amory, 1998, 45.
[19] Acton, 1984, v.
[20] Diana Mosley believed this story to be made up (*Loved Ones*, 1985, 104).

and places are often slightly altered so that, for example, Lady Berners becomes Lady Bourchier,[21] Mrs Foster becomes Mrs Farmer, Apley Park becomes Arley, and Cheam becomes Elmley. Other examples are found in his letters; in one to Cecil Beaton written in the early 1930s, he refers in passing to Lady Colefax as 'Lady Colebox'.[22]

First Childhood is perhaps the best place to begin an examination of Berners' character. He began work on it in September 1931, at the age of 48, and it is probable that he had delayed this until after the death of his mother in February of the same year. Perhaps her death caused him to reminisce – her home, Faringdon House, Berkshire, now became his permanent residence – but it is hardly surprising that he should have waited; few members of his family are spared criticism and his mother is no exception. In the chapter entitled 'My parents' he describes her and his father:

> My father was worldly, cynical, intolerant of any kind of inferiority, reserved and self-possessed. My mother was unworldly, naïve, impulsive and undecided, and in my father's presence she was always at her worst.[23]

Berners' mother had married Colonel Ward Bennitt in 1908, just a year after her first husband's sudden death (writing to her son to ask whether it would be permissible for her to remarry within a year, she began one letter, 'Knowing, as you do, how much I disliked your father...').[24] Bennitt died five weeks after Berners' mother in 1931, so by the time Berners began work on *First Childhood* all members of his immediate family who stood to be offended were dead. It was probably just as well: in one early passage Berners claims to have 'a shrewd suspicion that my grandfather's great wealth had some influence upon my father's choice [of bride]'.[25]

First Childhood deals with Berners' life up to the age of thirteen, and its great achievement is to convey details of his upbringing from the perspective of a child. Childhood being a time when trivial things assume an overwhelming importance, the book never becomes a dry account of the minutiae of life in the Tyrwhitt household but rather is filled with anecdotes

---

[21] Bourchier was actually the family name of one of Berners' distant relatives, Sir John Bourchier, the 1st Baron Berners, a great-grandson of Edward III, who took his wife's maiden name, Berners, for his barony.

[22] Amory, 1998, 128.

[23] 1934, 52.

[24] Amory, 1998, 43.

[25] 1934, 51.

and hilarious descriptions of the people who shaped his life. Nevertheless, the humour is, at times, hard pressed to disguise the bitterness he felt towards certain members of his family. Interestingly, *First Childhood* was not published until 1934; this was the longest period by far between the beginning of a literary work by Lord Berners and its eventual publication. By comparison, his six novels, which were published between 1936 and 1942, were all written in a matter of weeks.

Despite being primarily concerned with Berners' early life, many of the themes which recur throughout *First Childhood* were equally as important to him as an adult. One example is his attitude towards organised religion. The chapter headed 'The Bible-Throwing Episode' begins:

> The Bible, during my early years, failed to inspire me with the proper sentiments of reverence and affection. Indeed, I regret to say I even felt an active antipathy for the Holy Book, an attitude which was largely, if not entirely, the fault of my grandmother, Lady Bourchier.[26]

Much later in his life, Berners was still to have ambivalent feelings towards religion. During his most severe and prolonged breakdown at the beginning of the Second World War he wrote to Cecil Beaton:

> If I could find God I think it might help – but he seems to be very far off just now. I go to Pusey House every morning at eight o'clock in search of him and Penelope [Betjeman] has had a mass said for me at Uffington. This is serious. I wish I could find Him.[27]

Berners is unequivocal about whom he held responsible for his lack of religious conviction, laying the blame squarely on the shoulders of his paternal grandmother. He comments 'Poor Lady Bourchier!…If only her religion had proved some sort of consolation to her instead of merely serving to fill her soul with bitterness'.[28]

This antipathy towards his grandmother is one of the most striking admissions made in *First Childhood*. In another passage he states:

---

[26] Ibid., 228.
[27] Amory, 1998, 179.
[28] Berners, 1934, 45.

I feel sure that she must have been born with the seeds of a baleful asceticism in her heart, for not even conversion [to Roman Catholicism] could have succeeded in so permanently embittering any human being.[29]

By restricting the perimeters of his autobiographies so that they concern only his early life, Berners avoided having to disclose any of his adult anxieties and affairs. Despite the fact that he was exclusively homosexual, and spent the last eighteen years of his life living openly with Robert Heber Percy, a man almost thirty years his junior, the single reference to homosexuality in *First Childhood* is quickly dismissed. Details of his infatuation with an older pupil at 'Elmley' are presented in stark terms: 'His image haunted my waking thoughts and my dreams. Anything in the least way related to him, however commonplace, however trivial, was imbued with an almost celestial radiance.'[30] However, Berners distances himself from these comments by remarking: 'It has become a little difficult in these days of intensive sex-sophistication to write about school friendships, particularly of one between an older and a younger boy.'[31] 'I can only say that if my feelings towards Longworth were of a sexual nature I was certainly not aware of it at the time'.[32] It is not surprising that he did not wish to dwell too long on the subject: laws banning homosexual activity in Britain remained in force until 1967. Berners was essentially a private person who only expressed his feelings in the public sphere with a great deal of care, nevertheless his dedication at the beginning of *First Childhood* read: 'To Robert Heber-Percy Whose Knowledge of Orthography And Literary Style Has Proved Invaluable'. It was tongue in cheek – Heber Percy was no expert on orthography and literary style – but understood by those who knew the pair well.

Berners met the twenty-year-old Heber Percy[33] in 1932 and was immediately bowled over by him. He was later to document their meeting in his short, privately printed, novel *The Girls of Radcliff Hall*. Marguerite Radclyffe Hall (1883–1943) was a British novelist and poet who had achieved notoriety when her novel *The Well of Loneliness* (1928), which detailed a lesbian relationship, had been deemed obscene by a British judge. The book was banned, and only published in England over twenty years later, in 1949. Berners' novel, written in the style of the English

---

[29] Ibid., 37.
[30] Ibid., 212.
[31] Ibid., 212.
[32] Ibid., 212.
[33] 1911–1987.

author Angela Brazil,[34] characterised his homosexual acquaintances as girls in a boarding school of which he was the headmistress, Miss Carfax. Heber Percy, along with Oliver Messel, David Herbert, Peter Watson, Cecil Beaton and Robin Thomas, among others, were the pupils, each with crushes on the other girls. Most were at least mildly amused by Berners' portrayals, but Cecil Beaton – to whom image and social standing were acutely important – deplored the book and threatened to sue for libel. He is said to have gathered up copies and destroyed them.[35]

Frequently in *First Childhood* Berners does his best to show that he was an artist whose early life was dominated by philistines. Any opportunity to show how members of his family and people at his schools did their best to curb the imaginative and musical sides of his personality is taken and used as evidence. Whether this is a fair representation is impossible to say, however it is clear that having to contend with an overbearing grandmother, detached father, and often-preoccupied mother at home, as well as several sadistic teachers at school, must have contributed greatly to the enduring feelings of inadequacy he suffered throughout his life. His claim to be 'singularly free from complexes or repressions'[36] comes as something of a surprise in the face of the hostility he encountered, and the truth is rather that in later life he made a 'deliberate attempt to polish the surface and live on it'.[37] Significantly, however, it is the accounts of his battles against family and society that give *First Childhood* much of its humour. By way of contrast *A Distant Prospect*, in which Berners recalls details of his short but predominantly happy time at Eton, and *The Château de Résenlieu*, which concerns his enjoyable trip to Normandy after finishing at Eton, are far less entertaining.

It is perhaps inevitable that something so significant as his battle against depression would have an effect on Berners' art, but notably the only time it prevented him from composing was during his most severe breakdown at the start of the Second World War. Berners recalled this in his 1941 novel *Far from the Madding War*, when the wounds were still raw. The character Lord FitzCricket, mentioned above, provided the vehicle for Berners to describe his own sentiments towards the conflict:

---

[34] Angela Brazil (1868–1947) was an author of girls' books who wrote over forty school stories. Berners published *The Girls of Radcliff Hall* under the pseudonym Adela Quebec.
[35] Longer descriptions of the novel and Beaton's reaction are detailed in Amory (1998, 136–54) and Vickers (1993 ed., 171–79).
[36] Berners, *First Childhood*, 1934, 82.
[37] Amory, 1998, 36.

For a time the war knocked me out. I felt as if I had been pole-axed. I was unable to do anything at all...I couldn't compose music, I couldn't write or paint. It all seemed to have become so pointless. I believed it was the end of everything and certainly of people like me...I'm all the things that are no use in war. My character is essentially pacific and hedonistic. I like everything to be nice and jolly and I hate to think of people hating one another. I've never been any good at anything practical. I'm an amateur, and fundamentally superficial. I am also private spirited. I have never been able to summon up any great enthusiasm for the human race, and I am indifferent as to its future. I have always led a self-centred, sheltered life, and my little world consists of my hobbies and personal relationships.[38]

Fearing that introspection would be fatal, he kept it at bay by distancing himself from overly serious subject matter in his musical works. In music, as in life, he aimed to veer towards humour, vivacity and a wish to please, whilst deliberately avoiding profundity. Yet occasionally in his music we see glimpses of real compassion; Berners' appreciation of his need to avoid introspection left him able to sympathise with those in an equally gloomy state of mind. His depiction of the goldfish[39] in *Le poisson d'or*, for example, is not jovial in the least, but rather a heart-felt representation of the loneliness of a fish who longs for a companion. Perhaps only Lord Berners would have attributed the ability to feel so much genuine sorrow to a humble goldfish, but his choice of a character which other people would see as trivial, is revealing in itself. In the words of Berners' friend Constant Lambert, 'People realised that though his tongue was often in his cheek, his heart was just as frequently on his sleeve'.[40]

In addition to giving us a picture of the young Berners' home life, *First Childhood* offers some suggestions as to his early musical influences. We learn, for example, that he was first drawn to music through its visual characteristics – the look of the written music on the page – rather than its aural qualities, and that the first music to really capture his imagination was Chopin's *Fantaisie-Impromptu*. Interestingly there is nothing Chopinesque

---

[38] 1941, 129–30.

[39] In French, *Poisson rouge* is goldfish, *Poisson d'or* probably some type of ornamental koi carp. Debussy's 'Poissons d'or' (1907), which probably provided the idea for this piece, was inspired by a Chinese lacquerwork plaque in which the two swimming fish are certainly larger than goldfish. However, Berners' poem which heads the score mentions the fish swimming round and round in a bowl, suggesting that he does mean them to be goldfish.

[40] Steyn, 1983, 32.

about his own early piano music, although it may be significant that a great deal of his early compositions were works for solo piano.[41]

Berners' early fascination with the fantastic would also prove significant later on:

> I succeeded in amassing quite a substantial collection of fairy-story books, Grimm, Perrault, Madame d'Aulnoy, a volume of Russian folk-lore and an edition of the *Arabian Nights*…These books I used to devour with ecstatic enjoyment until at last I became completely engrossed in the fantastic world they chronicled.[42]

The plots of three of his ballets, *The Triumph of Neptune, Luna Park* and *Cupid and Psyche*, all concern fantasy characters. One, *Luna Park*, even has the sub-heading 'Fantastic ballet in one act'.

As will be shown in the next few chapters, Berners' musical style has much more in common with those of his French contemporaries and with Stravinsky than those of the 'nationalist' school of English composers which flourished in the early twentieth century. A word often used to describe his work is 'cosmopolitan', and it is clear that time spent living on the continent influenced his outlook on life and music. It would be wrong, however, to assume that connections with composers closer to home did not exist. William Walton's dedication of *Belshazzar's Feast* (1931) to Berners, mentioned above, was thanks for Berners' continued financial support of the younger composer (in this case, £50). Jointly with the Sitwells and the Dean of Christ Church Berners supported Walton in his early career with an annual income of £250.

During the second International Festival of Contemporary Music, held in Salzburg in 1923, Berners' *Valses Bourgeoises* and Walton's *String Quartet* were the only official British entries. When the pair met Berg and Schoenberg at the Festival Berners acted as interpreter in a discussion on composing at the piano. Three years later, when Berners was preparing *The Triumph of Neptune* for performance, Walton was asked to orchestrate four numbers, presumably to save time. As their careers progressed, though, the friendship waned, not as a result of any falling out, but because their musical activities were taking them in different directions. Then, in 1941, Berners wrote to Walton to assure him that a character in his novel *Far From the Madding War* – a composer called Francis Paltry – was not

---

[41] Although a late waltz written in 1943 is evidently a pastiche of Chopin's style.
[42] 1934, 26–27.

intended to be a portrait of him. In the novel, Paltry was dubbed 'the white
hope of English music', as Walton had been in real life, so other similarities
were bound to be sought. The rest of the characterisation, however, was
unkind:

> His compositions, though slightly lacking in originality and inclined to be long
> winded, were very much appreciated by the more serious of the English
> musical critics...He set out to get to know all the most influential musical
> authorities in the country...and made [his wife] ask them to luncheon.[43]

Berners' letter would have made Walton slightly uneasy even if he had
never read *Far from the Madding War*, but the whole affair was worsened
by Berners' additional claim to have saved his portrait of the composer for
another novel, *Count Omega*, to be published later that same year. In this
subsequent novel Emanuel Smith is a young composer desperate to make
his mark on the musical scene and obsessed with the idea of creating
something unique and vital to the world of music. He wants to re-establish
music as 'an essential and enduring part of the human soul',[44] and, struck
by a sudden creative urge, begins to write his first symphony. It is in a
single movement, and unsure as to how to finish it he enlists the help of a
gigantic trombonist, Gloria, the 'adopted daughter' of the mysterious title
character, Count Omega, to create a grand, breathtaking finale. In view of
Walton's struggle to find a suitable finale to his own first symphony,[45] the
joke was a little too close to home. Perhaps, too, Berners thought Walton
suffered from a lack of humour in both his attitude and his music, detecting
what Wilfrid Mellers would later brand 'the depressingly well-meaning
self-conscious Elgarizing in which Walton indulges'.[46]

   In his letter to Walton, Berners jokingly claimed to have had a solicitor
check his manuscript for anything libellous. Not appreciating the joke,
Walton contacted another solicitor who, in turn, wrote to Berners. Berners
was offended; Walton had been a little touchy, and Berners thought his
behaviour ungentlemanly, though the joke was decidedly mischievous, and
the characterisation unflattering.

---

[43] 1941, 50.
[44] Ibid., 174.
[45] Walton began work on his *Symphony No.1* in 1932, but progress was slow. He sanctioned
an incomplete performance of just the first three movements in December 1934 when the
finale was still unfinished. Finally completed in the summer of 1935, the symphony was
premiered in its entirety on 6 November 1935 under the baton of Sir Hamilton Harty.
[46] *Studies in Contemporary Music*, 1947, 182.

Constant Lambert (1905–51) was to be a firmer friend. On receiving a scholarship to the Royal College of Music, he had studied piano, composition under Vaughan Williams, Reginald Morris and George Dyson, and conducting under Malcolm Sargent. Also well known as a musicologist and conductor, Lambert had a lifelong association with English ballet which saw him become conductor of the Camargo Society Ballet on its foundation in February 1930.[47] When it became the Vic-Wells Ballet in 1931 Lambert was employed as musical director and remained there until 1947. He also conducted ballet and opera at Sadler's Wells, and became musical adviser there from 1948.

Lambert and Berners shared an admiration for Stravinsky and modern French composers and were the only two English composers to receive a commission from Diaghilev to write for the Ballets Russes: Berners for *The Triumph of Neptune* in 1926 (on which Lambert and Walton gave advice), and Lambert for *Romeo and Juliet*, produced in Monte Carlo in the same year. Evidently impressed by Berners' talents, Lambert wrote very favourably of him in his 1934 book *Music Ho! A Study of Music in Decline* and took an active role in promoting his music. When Berners' opera *Le carrosse du Saint-sacrement* received less than overwhelming critical acclaim Lambert assisted him in arranging the short orchestral interludes into an orchestral work *Caprice péruvien*. He also conducted the premieres of two of Berners' ballets, *A Wedding Bouquet* (1936) and *Cupid and Psyche* (1938–9), and helped with the setting of text for the chorus in *A Wedding Bouquet*. Performances of this choral ballet abroad replaced the chorus with a single narrator, Lambert,[48] who proved to be as ideal in this role as he had previously been in Walton's *Façade* (1921).[49] The two clearly had a great deal in common and their solid friendship lasted until Berners' death.

****

Though Lord Berners' career as a composer spanned a period of thirty-four years his musical style did not alter greatly with time. In another passage from *Far from the Madding War* Lord FitzCricket expresses concern about the English tendency 'to judge art by size and weight',[50] and

---

[47] Berners joined in December.
[48] See Chapter 6: The Ballets.
[49] Façade was dedicated to Lambert.
[50] 1941, 164.

the piano pieces, songs and few orchestral pieces written in the early stages of Berners' career reveal his preference for economy and directness of expression. After 1926 Berners turned his attentions almost exclusively to the larger-scale medium of ballet. However it is evident that one of the reasons ballet suited him is because it is a form which does not call for passages of lengthy musical development, and in this way the conciseness seen in his earlier works is still clear in these later ones. Ballet also appealed greatly to Lord Berners because of the importance of the visual element, and because it enabled him to collaborate with leading figures in the worlds of literature and art, in which he had a strong interest. The types of works he wrote also changed according to Berners' circumstances, so his earlier concentration on solo piano works and songs gave way to ballet when he became acquainted with Diaghilev, the choreographers Frederick Ashton and Georges Balanchine, and other ballet composers such as Constant Lambert.

The music of Lord Berners deserves reassessment; for the works of a composer who was so well-known and admired during his lifetime to have become almost completely neglected in the concert halls and theatres where they were first received with great success seems unduly harsh. At the time of the so-called English Musical Renaissance in the early decades of the twentieth century Lord Berners stood apart from the nationalist school of English composers who were seeking their inspiration in English heritage, poetry and folk-song. Berners was just as at home in France and Italy as he was in England and his cosmopolitan outlook is reflected in his music, whose originality and individuality of style contrasts markedly with many of his more celebrated English contemporaries. What other English composer of the time would have been comfortable setting song texts in French, German and English, or would have written an entire opera libretto in French? Though talented in many of the arts it was for his achievements as a composer that Lord Berners most wanted to be remembered. Now, more than half a century after his death, we should at least grant that wish to a man whose humour and taste for the exotic brought a breath of fresh air to English music.

Chapter 2

The Early Piano Music (1914–21)

The initial part of Lord Berners' career as a composer is dominated by piano music and songs. Despite being his first mature compositions the early piano works came to the attention of two highly influential figures, Stravinsky and Casella, whose commendation of Berners' musical talents was to have a significant effect on the direction of his career from that point. It was Casella who gave the first professional performance of Berners' music, when, on 30 March 1917, he played the *Trois petites marches funèbres* at the Academia Santa Cecilia. The encouragement Berners received for his early piano music gave him the confidence to tackle larger forces and bigger scale works, and these became the predominant interest in his later musical life.

Berners' early piano music of 1914–21 consists of eight works: *Dispute entre le papillon et le crapaud* (c.1914–15, published 1980), *Le poisson d'or* (1915, published 1919), *Trois petites marches funèbres* (1916, published 1917), *Fragments psychologiques* (1917, published 1919), *Valses bourgeoises* (1917, published 1919), *Trois morceaux* (1917, published as a piano duet in 1919, and for orchestra in 1921), *Portsmouth Point* (1918), and *Fantaisie espagnole* (1918, published separately as a piano duet and orchestral work in 1920). After these his attentions turned briefly towards short orchestral pieces and song before he became preoccupied with the larger mediums of opera and ballet. He returned to writing for the piano much later in his life, writing several pieces during the early 1940s.

Berners was largely self-taught both as a composer and pianist. He had extra music lessons when at Eton, and several orchestration lessons with the German composer Edmund Kretschmer[1] during his stay in Dresden in 1901, but other than that there is little evidence to indicate that he had any formal musical training. Very little is mentioned in his autobiographies and so it can be assumed that any early musical education he received was not particularly influential or inspiring. The first music to really capture the young Berners' imagination was Chopin's *Fantaisie-Impromptu*: hearing a

---

[1] Kretschmer (1830–1908) was organist of the Catholic Church in Dresden from 1854. He composed several operas including *Die Folkunger* (1875) which was one of the most successful of its day. In addition, he also wrote masses, a work for chorus and orchestra and another orchestral work.

relative play it for him when a child was sufficient to instil in him an interest in music which would remain with him throughout his life. At Eton he became fascinated with Wagner, and accounts in *A Distant Prospect* tell how he pored over copies of *Das Rheingold* and *Die Walküre*, even going so far as to transform an old dolls' house into a mini-theatre where he staged versions of these operas for members of his family. By his own accounts he was also a gifted improviser whose talents enabled him to entertain his Eton schoolmates whilst developing his creative imagination.

In his early piano music evidence of Berners' being self-taught as a pianist is not as abundant as might be expected, although there are passages in several pieces which suggest that his technique was unorthodox. Throughout these works there are no fingering markings and virtually no pedalling indications, suggesting that his primary concern was one of notation rather than practical performance. Perhaps there was a touch of laziness, too, *à la* Debussy. There are also frequent cases of music being written in a straight five-finger position (without passing the thumb under), as at the beginning of the *Dispute entre le papillon et le crapaud* (Ex. 2.1). The repeated sections in *Le poisson d'or* (Ex. 2.2) also suggest a brilliant if unorthodox personal technique, and in the second of the *Fragments psychologiques* a 'quasi glissando' fits conveniently into a ten-finger position (Ex. 2.3).

Ex. 2.1: *Dispute entre le papillon et le crapaud*, **bars 1–2**

Ex. 2.2: *Le poisson d'or*, **bars 18–19**

Ex. 2.3: *Fragments psychologiques No.2*, **'Le rire', bars 4–5**

Broadly speaking, Berners' musical style became more accessible throughout his career, and it is in these early piano pieces that it is at its most modern and obscure. The harmonic idiom of his early works is consistently chromatic and atonal; indeed the opening of his earliest completed (though not the first published) mature work, *Le poisson d'or*, consists entirely of evocative, non-functional chromatic progressions (Ex. 2.4).

Ex. 2.4: *Le poisson d'or*, **bars 1–2**

This work is of particular interest because of its extra-musical associations, indicated by the poem which heads the score. Written, in French, by Berners himself, this tells of the loneliness of the goldfish from the title:

> Morne et solitaire, le poisson d'or
> tournoie dans son bol de cristal.
> Il rêve une petite compagne, belle et brillante
> comme une pièce de vingt francs.......
> Mais, hélas! Quelque imbécile malavisé lui jette
> une miette de pain.
> L'image disparait dans l'eau trouble.
> Le poisson d'or avale sans joie la miette de pain
> et continue à tournoyer, morne et solitaire,
> dans son bol de cristal.

(Mournful and alone, the goldfish / circles in his crystal bowl. / He dreams of a little mate, beautiful and as shiny / As a twenty franc piece......./ But, alas! Some rash fool throws him / A crumb of bread. / The image fades into the murky water. / Joylessly the goldfish swallows the crumb of bread / and continues to circle, mournful and alone, / in his crystal bowl.)

Lane suggests that the music closely follows the poem by deriving ternary form from it,[2] and it is true that in both the poem and the score the opening material returns towards the end. However, in the music this is an exact repeat of the first eight bars, with a two-bar coda to finish, whereas in

---

[2] In CD liner notes to *Lord Berners Complete Vocal and Solo Piano Music*, Albany Records, TROY 290 (recorded 1994, issued 1997).

the poem the return to the 'A' section is less of an exact repeat, but rather a re-creation of the opening mood through the use of similar wording and ideas. Whether it is appropriate to label the intervening sixty bars of music a single 'B' section, though, is questionable: it begins with a contrasting rhythmic and melodic idea (see Ex. 2.2) but soon returns to material derived from the opening 'A' section.

    The use of a poem to head the score suggests that Berners had programmatic intentions for *Le poisson d'or*, and it might therefore be expected that the form would be largely dictated by the events of the poem. This is not entirely the case, however. There *is* a programmatic element, though whether Berners intended there to be precise references to the text is open to conjecture. Certain passages in the music are difficult to account for in this way; for example the *subito veloce* shown in Ex. 2.5 (bar 12) suggests a sudden and unexpected event but appears too early in the music to represent the crumb of bread being thrown into the bowl. The pentatonic, black-note glissando (Ex. 2.6), which appears shortly before the reprise of the opening music towards the end of the piece, is a far more likely candidate for an evocation of this particular event. We must assume, therefore, that the earlier *subito veloce* simply marks the beginning of the fish's dream, or some other event of which we are not told.

Ex. 2.5: *Le poisson d'or*, **bars 11–13**

Ex. 2.6: *Le poisson d'or*, **bars 67–69**

Accounting for every bar of music in this way is impossible because the poem and the music aim to create moods rather than relate events. Perhaps Berners had a more elaborate programme in mind when he completed his music, but felt it unnecessary or undesirable to detail it at the head of his score. To create too eventful an impression of the fish's life would be to undermine the portrayal of its monotonous and bleak existence. So although programmatic to a degree there is never the sense that the poem must account for all the events of the music.

The harmonies used by Berners further enhance his depiction of the goldfish, and although the chromatic progressions shown in Ex. 2.4 are non-functional, they admirably evoke the aimless activities of the fish. As he circles in his bowl so the music meanders around a recurring ascending chromatic scale. Contrary motion between the right and left hands, repeatedly moving apart and back together suggests the fish's circular movement, whilst creating the overall impression that there *is* movement, but it is within a limited sphere. There is none of the impetus that conventional harmonic progressions might confer; instead the atmosphere is an appropriately timeless one, punctuated by isolated dramatic moments. There is a vague prospect of the chromatic progressions leading towards a tonal centre, just as the fish has a dim hope that the mate he dreams of might one day materialise. A brief moment of optimism (Ex. 2.5), however, is soon banished and as the dream fades his perpetual melancholy existence comes back into view (see Ex. 2.2).

The title of Berners' work inevitably reminds the listener of Debussy's 'Poissons d'or' (1907) from *Images* for piano, and a comparison of the two pieces reveals how Berners was influenced by his more illustrious counterpart. In Debussy's work the fishes flick their tails against a background wash of demisemiquavers (see Ex. 2.7). In contrast, Berners' music is much more direct: he focuses attention on these tail flicks and there is no aquatic background to draw our attention away from the action. It is as though Debussy's music has been distilled down to its most active moments, and it is these that Berners takes as his starting point. The superficial similarities indicate that Berners knew his Debussy well, but his intention was to show how music had moved on in the intervening years. Indeed Berners' approach to the subject has more of the directness of expression of Stravinsky, with the flicks of the fish's tail being significantly on the beat in Ex. 2.4, rather than acting as anacruses, as in Ex. 2.7. The only suggestions of 'impressionism' come in the occasional pentatonic *glissandi* (see Ex. 2.6).

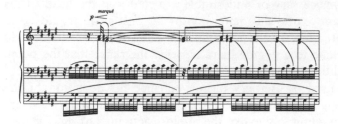

Ex. 2.7: Debussy: 'Poissons d'or', bars 3–4[3]

As in *Le poisson d'or*, Berners' aim in the *Dispute entre le papillon et le crapaud* ('Dispute Between the Butterfly and the Toad') is to use the music to illustrate the actions of the title characters. However, unlike *Le poisson d'or*, here the idea of a specific programme detailing actions rather than suggesting moods is more apparent; the only setback being that no indication of what the programme might actually be is given at the head of the score. Instead, Berners makes use of short passages of text inserted into the score at key moments as a partial narrative of events. The individual protagonists each have their own particular musical representation, the butterfly is suggested by the fluttering figure shown in Ex. 2.1 and the croaking, awkward toad by a jerky, leaping figure seen in Ex. 2.8. Characteristics of their music are combined to suggest interaction between them.

Ex. 2.8: *Dispute entre le papillon et le crapaud*, bars 5–6

Surprisingly, Berners never published the *Dispute*, which was only rediscovered at his Faringdon home during the 1970s. Lane suggests that Berners may have been wary of publishing because of the similarities between this work and Satie's *Sports et Divertissements* of 1914:[4] both use descriptive text throughout the musical score. However, it should be noted that Satie's work only appeared in print in 1923 and it is unlikely that

---

[3] Reproduced by kind permission of Editions Durand.
[4] In CD liner notes, op cit.

Berners would have seen it prior to publication.[5] It should also be observed that Satie uses text in a different way to Berners, as a running commentary to the music (see Ex. 2.9a), whereas Berners only employs it in a few places to highlight particular events (see Ex. 2.9b). The way the text appears on the score also differs: Satie's text permeates the music like a prose poem, whereas Berners inserts his at isolated strategic moments. Notably, the use of a programme in this and *Le poisson d'or* is also far more in keeping with Satie than with Debussy. It is possible, too, that this is simply an early work which Berners did not consider good enough to publish. In certain ways it seems less accomplished than *Le poisson d'or*: it is much shorter, and the juxtapositions of the butterfly's and toad's music are never quite convincing, seeming at times rather like a compositional exercise. However, the harmonic idiom of both works is similar, suggesting that the two were not written years apart. All that is really clear is that if Berners had been reluctant to publish at the time it was written, he would have been even less inclined to do so later in his career when he had rejected his early venture into atonalism in favour of a more accessible style.

Ex. 2.9a: Satie, 'La Pêche' from *Sports et Divertissements*[6]

Ex. 2.9b: *Dispute entre le papillon et le crapaud*, bars 9–11

Berners' next work for piano solo, the *Trois petites marches funèbres*, was completed in 1916 and was the first in which his droll humour really became apparent. The title of each march gives an indication that these are no conventional funereal laments: 'Pour un homme d'état', 'Pour un canari'

---

[5] Though as he purchased copy no.13 he must have been quick to obtain it.
[6] Reproduced by kind permission of Editions Salabert, Paris/United Music Publishers Ltd.

and 'Pour une tante à l'héritage'.[7] The first march is headed *Très lent et pompeux* and from the outset Berners signals that the statesman's death has given those who knew him little reason to grieve. It begins with a *fortissimo* nod to Beethoven's Fifth Symphony, but the chord which follows the reiterated quavers is unexpectedly major rather than Beethoven's minor (by implication) and is followed by a low register chromatic quip (Ex. 2.10). Similar grace-note jibes appear throughout, challenging the stoical nature of the occasion by underlining its inherent humour. Berners was unimpressed by those with pretensions of grandeur, and in this first march this is readily apparent. References to the opening motive abound, but the emptiness of the reiterated unison chords only emphasises further the mock sincerity of the event.

Ex. 2.10: 'Pour un homme d'état', bars 1–2

The third funeral march is similarly unconventional. Titled 'Pour une tante à l'héritage', it is translated into English in the score as 'For a Rich Aunt' but Berners also suggested an alternative, 'For an aunt with a legacy', on his manuscript copy. Implications are that the death of the aunt is a cause for celebration – the music is headed *Allegro giocoso* – and a jocular spirit is evident from the opening, where there is a sense of unfettered delight, with sequential staccato semiquaver figures (Ex. 2.11) rippling like waves of laughter. The excitement builds up throughout, becoming more and more frenetic towards the end until the final gleeful descent to finish triumphantly on a *ffff sfz* chord.

---

[7] Berners re-used these three pieces in his puppet ballet *L'Uomo dai baffi* (1918). The titles were changed to 'The Blue Ballerina', 'The Drunken Dancer' and 'The Tip-Toeing White Mice'. The ballet, which was arranged for chamber ensemble by Alfredo Casella, also featured arrangements of the *Fragments psychologiques* and *Portsmouth Point*. See Appendix 2.

Ex. 2.11: 'Pour une tante à l'héritage', bars 1–2

In true 'contrariwise' Berners fashion, the only one of the marches which displays any real sense of grief is the second, 'For a canary'. Persistent twitters are heard throughout this heart-felt lament, and are not mock sentimentality but genuine sadness (Ex. 2.12). Lane suggests these are 'ghostly chirpings from the deceased bird',[8] but the fact that they are marked *incisivo, marcarto il canto* suggests that these are rather the mournful chirps of his companions. Berners' original design for the cover of this work shows six canaries carrying the coffin of their dead friend and it is surely these companions who chirp their tribute here.

Ex. 2.12: 'Pour un canari', bars 1–4

A sombre and steady beat marks this funeral procession, whilst above it a slow and marked chromatic melody unfolds, extending over a limited range of six notes. Throughout most of the piece the chirps are noticeable for their high pitch which contrasts with the lower melody. An answering phrase, higher in register, follows and leads to a passage marked *singhiozzando* ('sobbing'), in which the new theme is woven into a fugato above which the chirps are silent. At the end there is a return to the mournful music of the opening, but with the melody transposed down an augmented second. The last chord remains unresolved, but is followed by a final chirp from one of the grieving canaries (Ex. 2.13). The genuine sense of melancholy in 'Pour un canari' reminds us of the compassion Berners showed for the goldfish in *Le poisson d'or* and makes us wonder whether he preferred animals to people!

---

[8] In CD liner notes, op cit.

Ex. 2.13: 'Pour un canari', bars 33–34

In the same year that he completed his *Trois petites marches funèbres*, Berners wrote another set of three pieces for piano solo, perhaps following Satie's penchant for such groupings. These were his *Fragments psychologiques*, individually titled 'La haine' (Hatred), 'Le rire' (Laughter) and 'Un soupir' (A sigh). Representing basic human impulses in music was one of Berners' more ambitious projects and 'La haine' contains some of the most desolate music he ever wrote. Both laughter and sighing are physical acts which make them easier to suggest by imitation in music; hatred is an emotion, which by definition is much more difficult to evoke in this way. The incredible bleakness of 'La haine' is largely due to its complex tonality; it is one of the most harmonically obscure of Berners' piano works. Here he goes beyond chromaticism towards polytonality. The opening, for example, begins with juxtaposed C-minor and G-sharp diminished chords followed by an ascending run of chromatic minor triads in the left hand (Ex. 2.14):

Ex. 2.14: 'La haine' bars 1–2

The low register, thickly textured chords together with their deliberate, accented ascent create a sombre atmosphere, and the opening chord, which is reiterated at the beginning of each of the first four bars, tolls ominously in the foreground. This chord is not heard again until the final four bars of 'La haine' when it re-emerges in the *Primo movimento*. Here the opening music returns, but now in a shadowy form, *piano*, punctuated by two sudden *sforzandi* outbursts, before the sound gradually dies away to an unresolved *pianissimo*, suggesting that attempts at reconciliation have proved fruitless.

Phrases throughout 'La haine' tend to be short, invariably contain chromatic movement and often build up with a crescendo. Brief rests appear within or between phrases, hampering the natural musical progression and creating a feeling of fragmentation which suggests that though anger is being consciously suppressed, turbulent emotions still bubble just under the surface. Chromatic progressions, usually contained in the upper part of the right hand line, are a constant feature. These vary in length; one extends through six bars of music from the B below middle C to the first A above the treble stave, but is cleverly disguised by melodic interest in the left hand which draws attention away from the chromatic line at the top of 'accompanying' right hand chords. Perhaps the task of incorporating such a lengthy chromatic line without drawing attention to it was an exercise or challenge that Berners set himself. By using such chromaticism along with sudden plunges in the melodic line (see Ex. 2.15), Berners steers clear of 'comfortable' harmonic and melodic progressions which might undermine the overall effect of revulsion and contempt that he is aiming to create.

Ex. 2.15: 'La haine', bars 11–12

The dynamic structure of 'La haine' further enhances the sense of extreme unease which pervades the piece. There are sustained *fortissimo* passages, with crashing leaps, such as shown in Ex. 2.16, and crescendos building up to *fff* and even *ffff* with repeated, thick, accented chords. Importantly, though, there are *subito piano* and *pianissimo* markings in the central section which bring another dimension to the piece. Here the feelings of hatred are kept more closely under control, and the mood contrasts sharply with the violently felt disgust of the outer sections. In addition to the enormous dynamic range there are also many different textures and the strong contrasts of these elements serve to translate the intensity and extremeness of 'hatred' into musical terms. Our sense of stability is frequently further undermined when harmonic progressions are interrupted before reaching a conclusion, and when crescendos build up slowly but suddenly die away. With these effects Berners indicates the intrinsic absurdity and irrationality of hatred as he sees it.

Ex. 2.16: 'La haine', bars 9–10

The second of the *Fragments*, 'Le rire', is a complete change of mood from 'La haine'. Heavy accented low chords are replaced by lighter, higher staccato ones and the cartoon-like depiction of laughter echoes his earlier funeral march 'Pour une tante à l'héritage'. Exx. 2.17a and b show passages from both pieces in which these similarities are obvious. The repeated staccato chords create an onomatopoeic impression of laughter. There are *sforzandi* and sudden changes of dynamics throughout which remind us of Berners' descriptions of 'perilous laughter' – laughter which must be suppressed at all costs – in *First Childhood*.[9]

Ex. 2.17a: 'Pour une tante a l'héritage', bars 24–25

Ex. 2.17b: 'Le rire', bar 3

The last piece of the set, 'Un soupir' is stylistically similar to the other two, with sliding chromaticism and bitonality both prevalent once again. As with 'Le rire', the title here provides something tangible which can be imitated in the music, and the musical characterisation of a sigh provides the basis for the whole piece. Lane suggests that a sigh would usually be heard of as a downward gesture, and that Berners' use of a chromatic rise and fall suggests 'a wistful rather than regretful yearning'.[10] It seems more likely,

---

[9] 1934, 44.
[10] In CD liner notes, op cit.

however, that the rise and fall – which is referred to throughout the entire piece – simply suggests the intake and exhalation of breath that constitutes a sigh. This particular figure appears in the right hand, and underneath the left hand supports by moving in the opposite direction; after its first chord it leaps down two octaves before working its way up through part of a chromatic scale in thirds (see Ex. 2.18). Pauses between the short (usually two-bar) phrases, combined with altered rhythmic patterns at the ends of the phrases, give the piece a feeling of timelessness and ensure that there is no suggestion of regularity about the sighs. The opening material reappears in a *Tempo primo* towards the end and is heard again in the final four bars, now *ppp* becoming *pppp* an octave higher. The dynamic level in 'Un soupir' never rises above *piano* and it always seems to describe introspection, a personal moment of longing, rather than an outward signal of dissatisfaction.

Ex. 2.18: 'Un soupir' bars 1–4

Two years after completing the *Fragments psychologiques* Berners was to return to the piano for another work, *Portsmouth Point*. The title inevitably provokes comparisons with Walton's overture of the same name, and it is significant that Berners completed his piano score some seven years before Walton began work on his overture. The inspiration, however, a print by the English painter and caricaturist Thomas Rowlandson (1756–1827), was the same. Renowned for his illustrations of eighteenth century English life, Rowlandson inspired the two composers with a print showing a crowded Portsmouth waterfront scene, in which a fleet prepares to depart. Considering that Berners and Walton were (at this stage of their careers) mutually supportive, it is likely that Walton would have been aware of Berners' work. Perhaps Berners even inspired Walton to investigate Rowlandson's scene.

Originally intending to write a ballet, Berners first completed a piano solo, which he later began to orchestrate. The orchestration, however, only progressed for fifty bars before Berners abandoned the idea. Perhaps the need to extend the piece significantly was too daunting a task for someone who, at that point, had only completed short piano works and songs.

Although one of his longest piano works at a shade under four minutes, *Portsmouth Point* would clearly need to have been expanded if to provide the basis for a ballet. Also it is worth noting that Berners' experience of orchestration was limited and his first completed ballet, *The Triumph of Neptune*, was not begun until he had some experience of writing for larger scale forces (see Chapter 4). It is interesting, though, that Berners' attraction to ballet went back this far. If the lack of experience in handling orchestral forces and extended musical forms were not good enough reason for Berners to abandon his orchestration of *Portsmouth Point* it is clear that 1918 – the year in which Berners inherited the barony – would have been quite busy enough! An instrumental version of the work *was* made in 1918, but not by Berners. Alfredo Casella arranged several of Berners' piano pieces, including *Portsmouth Point*, for a puppet ballet, *L'Uomo dai baffi* ('The Man with the Moustache') performed in Rome on 15 April 1918 by a puppet theatre group, Balli Plastici, in a concert organised by the futurist set Fortunato Depero. The ballet comprised *Portsmouth Point*, *Trois morceaux* and *Trois petites marches funèbres*, which were given new names,[11] and scored for an instrumental ensemble consisting of a flute, oboe, clarinet in A, bassoon, piano and strings.

It was the vitality of the busy, crowded scene that Berners and Walton both captured in their interpretations of Rowlandson's print. Like much of Berners' earlier piano music *Portsmouth Point* is divided into short sections which are littered with repeated motives. It is lively and discordant with wide-leaping thick chords. The music progresses from one section to another in different ways, either ending abruptly then beginning again after a brief silence, or by merging seamlessly. This reflects the ways that a painting can be viewed: the eye may focus on one part, blink, then move and refocus on a different section, or else scan the canvas in a more smooth movement. Written at a time when Berners was very much in awe of Stravinsky the score contains, perhaps not surprisingly, very strong echoes from *The Rite of Spring* (particularly the 'Jeux des cités rivales').

Perhaps because he intended to orchestrate *Portsmouth Point*, and therefore did not feel that it was properly finished, Berners never published the solo piano version. Certainly, after the success of Walton's overture of the same name, premiered in 1926, it would have been difficult for Berners to use the title for a ballet or even to publish the piano version. This remains a great pity because it is one of the most lively and captivating of his early works. Perhaps the issuing of a 1997 recording[12] may be followed by a publication. Berners, after all, had the idea first!

---

[11] See Appendix 2.
[12] *Lord Berners: The Complete Vocal and Solo Piano Works*. Albany records, TROY 290, 1997.

In addition to his works for solo piano, Berners also completed several piano duets during the early part of his career as a composer. These were *Valses bourgeoises* (a set of three waltzes individually entitled 'Valse brillante', 'Valse caprice', and 'Strauss, Strauss, et Straus'), *Trois morceaux* (individually headed 'Chinoiserie', 'Valse sentimentale' and 'Kasatchok'), and *Fantaisie espagnole*. Of these the *Trois morceaux* and *Fantaisie espagnole* were also published as orchestral works. Establishing which format is the original in these cases is not straightforward because, unfortunately, the dates of publication give no confirmation of the order in which the different formats were completed. In the case of the *Trois morceaux*, for example, the orchestral version (under the title 'Three Pieces for Orchestra') was published in 1921, two years after the version for piano duet appeared in print. However, the orchestral work was premiered in 1919, two years before it was published. The most likely explanation is that Berners sketched each work at the piano, and used this sketch as the basis for his orchestration. Then, as was typical of the time, the final piano duet versions were arranged from the orchestral works, although there is no explicit proof of this.[13] It is also conceivable that he completed the different formats concurrently, although, again, there is no evidence to support this. The *Trois morceaux* will be examined in this chapter, *Fantaisie espagnole* in Chapter 4. *Trois morceaux* is included here because the style of writing is very similar to Berners' other early piano music; the five-finger position writing mentioned earlier, and also seen in Berners' songs (see Chapter 3), is very much in evidence in each of the three movements, unlike *Fantaisie espagnole* which, in contrast, is written idiomatically for the instruments used in the orchestral version.

Berners completed the *Valses bourgeoises* in 1917, between the solo piano works *Trois petites marches funèbres* and *Portsmouth Point*. Unlike his later *Trois morceaux* and *Fantaisie espagnole*, he never produced an orchestral arrangement of these waltzes, which is surprising in view of the fact that they have much in common with the other piano duets, which *did* appear in orchestral versions.[14] In these waltzes Berners aimed to hark back to earlier times, an intention evident from the elaborately stylised front cover as well as from the music itself.

---

[13] It should be noted that in the inside cover of one edition of Berners' piano duet *Valses bourgeoises* the publishers, J & W Chester, have included a list of all available music written by Berners. This includes the piano duet versions of the *Trois morceaux* and *Fantaisie espagnole*, next to which is written 'Transcription by the Composer'.

[14] Philip Lane completed an orchestrated version of the *Valses bourgeoises* for a 1996 recording (*Lord Berners: The Triumph of Neptune*, Marco Polo, 8.223711. Recorded 1996, issued 1998).

The waltzes are intentionally full of musical clichés, but are distinguished by unmistakable Berners touches. Conventional waltz motives are used throughout, but are slightly altered, forcing the listener to question how something can sound so familiar and yet not quite 'right' at the same time. An example is the continuous 'oom-pah-pah' bass figure in the 'Valse brillante' which continues for the first forty bars, irrespective of the fact that the prima part above does not quite seem to fit against it. The first twelve bars are shown in Ex. 2.19. In all three of the waltzes, figures which do not sit easily against one another are nevertheless forced into juxtaposition; the listener at first winces at the jarring clashes of what seem to be wrong notes, but soon becomes accustomed to the discordant nature of the music.

Ex. 2.19: 'Valse brillante', bars 1 – 8

Lane remarks on an 'obvious allusion' in the 'Valse brillante' to the 'Marche of the Davidsbündler' from Schumann's *Carnaval*,[15] but the similarities mainly arise only from a similar dotted-crotchet – quaver – crotchet rhythm, and a swooping quaver gesture shown in Exx. 2.20a and b. It is fairer to say that 'Valse brillante' is an imitation of nineteenth century piano waltzes than to attempt to locate specific models in this way.

---

[15] In CD liner notes to *Lord Berners: The Triumph of Neptune, L'Uomo dai baffi, Valses bourgeoises, Polka*, Marco Polo 8.223711. Recorded 1996, issued 1998, 8.

Ex. 2.20a: 'Valse brillante', Primo part, bars 59–62

Ex. 2.20b: Schumann, 'Marche des Davidsbündler contre les Philistins' from *Carnaval*, Op.9, bars 94–98[16]

The same idea is used throughout 'Valse caprice': fully aware of what we expect to hear, Berners manipulates us from start to finish, tantalisingly alluding to familiar tunes, but avoiding them by using 'wrong' or 'off-key' notes. Ex. 2.21 shows one example in which a familiar waltz motive is transformed through the use of accidentals which first appear in the second bar. What we expect to hear as a neatly descending sequence in the right hand is thrown off course, and the phrase ends up on an A instead of the anticipated G. The left hand, meanwhile, carries blithely on with an 'oom-pah-pah' bass, remaining resolutely in the 'correct' key.

Ex. 2.21: 'Valse caprice', Secondo part, bars 27–30

The third and final waltz, 'Strauss, Strauss et Straus' (Johann, Richard and Oscar, respectively) contains the most obvious allusion to another work, Richard Strauss' *Der Rosenkavalier* (see Ex. 2.22). Where this appears Berners writes above the score, 'Mais je connais ça', revealing to the listener that this really is intended as an affectionate imitation.

---

[16] Reproduced by kind permission of Peters Edition Limited, London.

Ex. 2.22: 'Strauss, Strauss et Straus', bars 26–31

The *Trois morceaux* were completed in 1917, though not published until 1919, and were dedicated respectively to Michel Larionow, who designed the title pages in the Chester publication for piano duet, Eugene Goossens and Natalia Gontcharowa, who had designed the cover for *Le poisson d'or*. These were Berners' first exercises in pastiche composition: ones in which he deliberately set out to imitate other musical styles. He had a natural aptitude for such writing, leading Constant Lambert to refer to the 'brilliant parodies of Lord Berners' in his 1934 book *Music Ho!*.[17] Berners' aim was not to mock other people's work, but rather to create a cordial homage to composers or styles he admired, and it was because he had a genuine fondness for the music he imitated that the results were so successful.

The Oriental flavour in the first piece of the set, 'Chinoiserie' is reminiscent of Weber's *Turandot* (1809) and Sullivan's *Mikado* (1885), and is so successfully achieved that it is surprising to discover that the scales Berners uses are not strictly pentatonic. An Eastern quality emerges, at the beginning, for example, through the use of prominent perfect fourths and fifths in both Primo and Secondo parts. The pentatonic scale D, E, G, A, B, is prevalent but is not used exclusively: Ex. 2.23 shows an early melody in which the non-pentatonic notes are marked with asterisks.

Ex. 2.23: 'Chinoiserie', Primo part, bars 7–14

---

[17] 1934, 192.

Berners' view of the Orient as a vibrant, bustling place is evident from the beginning of 'Chinoiserie'. A fast staccato figure is repeated in the Secondo part (see Ex. 2.24) and similar quaver movement continues throughout much of the piece. In this particular example the right hand notes belong to the pentatonic scale named above, but the repeated C naturals in the left hand do not.

Ex. 2.24: 'Chinoiserie', Secondo part, bars 1–4

Piano duet form allows Berners to use extreme contrasts of register, and to build up the sound in a much more dramatic way than in a piece for solo piano. He uses similar techniques to vary the texture of the music as he does in his solo piano works, only now the contrasts are even more marked. Themes are passed between parts or used in a 'question-and-answer' format so that the left hand of the Secondo might answer a motif posed by the right hand of the Primo. Excitement builds up towards the end of 'Chinoiserie' when themes are shortened and repeated in rapid succession at different pitches. Increasing dynamic levels and thicker textures also intensify the feeling of driving energy in the final bars. The final chord, as is the case with each of the three pieces in the set, seems not to be the one we expect, and as such the facetious character of Lord Berners manages to prevail even when he is imitating others.

The title of the second piece in this set, 'Valse sentimentale' immediately suggests a connection with Ravel's *Valses nobles et sentimentales* (1911) and it soon becomes evident that the second of Ravel's eight waltzes has provided the inspiration behind this work. In Ravel's waltz an introductory passage sets the mood, creating an atmosphere of veiled harmonic mystery out of which the first theme gently emerges. The introduction to Berners' piece bears a distinct resemblance to this first theme of Ravel's, and when the Primo begins in the fifth bar it plays chords with added sevenths, ninths and raised elevenths which could have come directly from the pen of Ravel. One particular chord – an augmented triad (G, B, D sharp) – appears in both works. The mood, harmonies and gentle lilting rhythm of Berners' *Lento* cannot fail to remind us of the opening of Ravel's waltz. Berners takes two passages from Ravel – the opening chord introduction, and a melodic figure from bar 9 – and

forges them together so that they are played *at the same time* from bar 5
onwards. Exx. 2.25a – c clarify these points, with Ex. 2.25c showing
Berners' addition of a wide-leaping bass staccato idea. This transformation
of Ravel's gentle rising octaves into what looks like a Stravinskian bass
ostinato was surely intended as a parody.

Ex. 2.25a: Ravel, *Valses nobles et sentimentales*, No.II, bars 1–5[18]

Ex. 2.25b: Ravel, *Valses nobles et sentimentales*, No.II, bars 9–12[19]

Though the similarities are so marked, it seems to be Berners' aim during
the course of his 'Valse sentimentale' also to highlight the differences
between his approach and that of Ravel. There are changes of mood which
do not appear in Ravel's waltz, and when the opening theme returns in the
Piu lento, the Primo part's left hand supporting chords owe little to the
French composer (see Ex. 2.26). It is as if the piece began as 'Ravel by
Berners' and ends purely as 'Berners by Berners'. Both this bitonality and
the Stravinskian ostinato mentioned above bring the piece bang up to date
in a witty and original way, using familiar models in unexpected guises or
combinations.

---

[18] © Editions Durand.
[19] © Editions Durand.

Ex. 2.25c: Berners 'Valse sentimentale', bars 1–8

Ex. 2.26: 'Valse sentimentale', Primo part, bars 63–65

In the third piece of the set, 'Kasatchok', Berners' attention is directed towards Russian folk music. Headed *Allegro feroce*, this is a wild stomp through two Russian-inspired melodies. The first is shown in Ex. 2.27, and appears at the top of the right hand chords in the Secondo part.

Ex. 2.27: 'Kasatchok', Secondo part, bars 9–10

'Kasatchok' owes a huge debt to Stravinsky's *The Rite of Spring*; though it has none of the rhythmic complexity of the *Rite*, the energy and driving force which propels it forward is very similar. The second main folk-like theme actually resembles one from the 'Cercles mystérieux des adolescentes' from part two of the *Rite*, as Exx. 2.28a and b show:

Ex. 2.28a: 'Kasatchok', Primo part, bars 46–49

Ex. 2.28b: *The Rite of Spring*, **'Cercles mystérieux des adolescentes', alto flute part, bars 13–18**[20]

Although Berners' first piano works were his earliest compositions they represented the distinctive voice of a fully-fledged cosmopolitan composer who arrived on the European musical scene during the early years of the twentieth century. Despite the fact that these works were written at the beginning of Berners' career as a composer, and were written within a space of five years, recognisable traits distinguish an idiosyncratic musical style which remained more or less unchanged throughout his work from then on.

One of the most instantly noticeable features of his piano music, for example, is its brevity, though it is fairer to think of these works as concentrated rather than simply short. Often the music is divided into concise sections or phrases which do not develop but examine different aspects of a single idea through variation. The progression from one section to another is entirely logical, if not always anticipated, and the result is one of a satisfying formal balance. The larger-scale of the ballets which dominated his later career did not prevent this particular characteristic from remaining present in his work; in fact it is clear that one reason ballet as a medium particularly suited him is because of its sectional nature.

Berners' form of expression throughout the early piano music is direct and to the point, and to this end the carefully chosen titles of each work play a vital role in focusing our attention on what is being expressed. In the *Trois petites marches funèbres* the titles allow us to appreciate further the inherent humour of 'Pour un homme d'état' and 'Pour une tante à l'héritage'. The listener is 'primed' by the titles and as a result the music is made even more effective.

---

[20] Text reproduced by permission of Boosey & Hawkes Music Publishers Ltd.

All the music for solo piano from this point in Berners' career concerns states of the human condition. Even when the title characters are not human (*Le poisson d'or*, *Dispute entre le papillon et le crapaud*, 'Pour un canari') anthropomorphic treatment attributes to them human emotions of loneliness, anger, indignation or despair. In the *Trois petites marches funèbres* we can compare the variations in emotive response which the deaths of different characters provoke, and in the *Fragments psychologiques* we are shown direct musical representations of hatred, glee and melancholia. In contrast, the piano duets move away from such characterisations and focus more on the imitation of different musical styles. The duets are also significantly longer than the solo piano works, perhaps evidence that they were originally conceived as orchestral works.

In the solo piano music Berners' harmonic idiom tends to be chromatic with leanings towards bitonality or even polytonality. In the duets the style is slightly more tonal, and chromaticism is used for effect rather than as a starting point. Many of the solo works, in particular, contain sudden dynamic contrasts and passages in which there are swift changes between widely contrasting registers. Melodic lines tend to include sudden swoops provoking certain critics to suggest that Berners could not write a tune. Nevertheless, his music was widely acclaimed by many leading musicians of the time, and as a result he was encouraged to continue composing and to go on to experiment with other genres.

A sense of irony is often present, and frequently it seems as though Berners is deliberately aiming to provoke. This aspect of his work reflects Berners' personality as revealed in his autobiographies and through the writings of those who knew him; finishing pieces flippantly with an almost 'thrown-away' ending is another example. This demonstrates, above all, that he was a composer who composed primarily for *himself* rather than for other people. He was not trying to please others or to impress them, but was simply allowing himself to write music which entertained him. Perhaps later generations misinterpreted this self-sufficiency for egotism, which might explain why Berners' music was neglected for so many years after his death.

Chapter 3

The Early Songs (1913–21)

Lord Berners' songs were mainly completed during the early part of his composing career, with the majority being finished between 1920 and 1921. There are four sets of three songs: *Lieder Album – Three songs in the German manner* (1913–18, published 1920), *Trois chansons* (1920, published 1921), *Three English Songs* (1920, published 1920), *Three Songs* (1921, published 1921), and one single song, *Dialogue Between Tom Filuter and his Man by Ned the Dog Stealer* (1921, published 1924). Names of individual songs from the sets are listed in Appendix 2.

The period of five years that he took to complete the *Lieder Album* was unusually lengthy for Berners. Although the reasons for this are not documented, it is likely that upheavals in his personal life – he inherited the barony in 1918 after the deaths of his grandmother and uncle – might have interrupted their progress. Perhaps, too, the fact that he was starting out in a new and unfamiliar genre prompted Berners to spend so much time over these first songs. Most likely, though, is that an interest in writing for solo piano took over at that time, especially after Stravinsky's approval of his early work *Le poisson d'or* (1915). The other sets of songs were completed much more quickly, and it is significant that they were written after his early solo piano music had been published and after he had given up his job at the embassy. The piano music had helped bring his compositional style to the attention of influential musical figures; once they had persuaded him to devote more time to composition he was able to complete several works within a relatively short time. Although his anthology of vocal music was by no means large, the songs, with texts in English, French and German, helped establish Berners as a truly cosmopolitan composer. Significantly, he used the word-setting skills he acquired at this time in his 1922 opera *Le carrosse du Saint-sacrement* (with libretto by Berners)[1] and in his 1936 choral ballet *A Wedding Bouquet*.

Completed so soon after his early piano works, Berners' vocal music could be expected to contain characteristics of his piano writing, especially

---

[1] Berners' opera was begun in 1920, but he is likely to have completed most of the *Trois chansons* and *Three English Songs*, which date from the same year, before beginning the larger scale project.

in their accompaniments. Examination of the vocal scores shows this to be the case, and it is these similarities which will be considered first. As the previous chapter has shown, there are numerous features in Berners' piano writing which occur frequently enough to be regarded as characteristic of his early style. Satiean brevity and directness of expression, for example, are idiosyncratic, as is the way musical ideas do not develop but are altered through variation. These qualities are just as evident in the songs, whose average length is only thirty-six bars. (The average length of the early music for solo piano is forty-one bars.)

Evidence of the piano accompaniments being written in a five-finger position (without passing the thumb under) abounds in the songs, as it does in the solo piano music. Particularly characteristic are staccato or accented passages in which the hands move up or down the keyboard in five-finger positions without needing to retain a legato line (cf. Exx. 3.1 and 2.1, bar 1). Glissandos are also usually divided between the hands so that each can remain in a five-finger position: Exx. 3.2 and 2.3 show quasi glissandos in 'König Wiswamitra' from the *Lieder Album* and 'Le rire' from *Fragments psychologiques*.

Ex. 3.1: 'König Wiswamitra', bars 26–27

Ex. 3.2: 'König Wiswamitra', bars 29–30

In 'La fiancée du timbalier' from *Trois chansons* the 'annoyingly off-centre'[2] military opening is typically Berners in style (Ex. 3.3a); frequently in the early piano music Berners combines themes which do not quite 'go together' in this way. This particular example has clear similarities with a passage from the 'Prélude' to Debussy's *La boîte à joujoux* (1913, published 1913), in which identical Stravinskian thirds descend chromatically (Ex. 3.3b, bars 45–46). Debussy, like Berners, uses a fanfare figure ('*Gentiment militaire*'), but here it appears before the descending thirds, rather than simultaneously with them. Debussy's military theme is diatonic, with bitonal implications arising from the supporting harmony; Berners takes this a stage further by using notes from an octatonic pitch collection (III in Ex. 3.3c) in his melody above the chromatically descending bass. Berners seems to use the Debussy passage as a model, upon which he stamps his own unmistakably modern mark.

Ex. 3.3a: 'La fiancée du timbalier', bars 1–5

Ex. 3.3b: Debussy 'Prélude' to *La boîte à joujoux*, (piano reduction) bars 44–47[3]

---

[2] Lane: CD liner notes to *Lord Berners: Complete Vocal and Solo Piano Music*, Albany Records, TROY 290 (recorded 1994, issued 1997).
[3] Reproduced by kind permission of Editions Durand.

Ex. 3.3c: Octatonic pitch collections[4]

The technique of using octatonic pitch collections – eight-note scales consisting of alternating tone-semitone intervals[5] – is not unusual in Berners' music; although none of his songs or piano pieces are exclusively octatonic, there are often several examples like the one above within each piece. These are most often small sections found within a larger phrase although there are several passages in which a particular octatonic pitch collection is used more extensively. Ex. 3.1, for example shows bars 26–27 of 'König Wiswamitra', and, with the exception of the G sharp in the piano in the upbeat to bar 26, all the notes are taken from collection III shown above. This is used in the following three bars, too, which end the piece, although a *quasi glissando*, which includes non-octatonic notes, slides down onto the final note.

Berners persistently delights in surprising the listener, and one way he achieves this in both the solo piano music and songs is by using a sudden and unexpectedly wide leap in the piano, as Exx. 3.4 and 2.16 demonstrate. In this way the full range of the piano is used to striking effect.

Ex. 3.4: 'L'étoile filante', bars 10–12

---

[4] As classified in Van Den Toorn, P, *The Music of Igor Stravinsky*, 1983, 51.
[5] C sharp may also appear as D flat, F sharp as G flat, and so on.

Throughout the early piano music Berners' modernity is displayed by the ease with which he uses chromaticism. Invariably a starting point rather than an inspired afterthought, it never seems inappropriate in his music, and is as integral a part of the songs as it is of the early piano pieces. Berners rejects the opportunity to give the voice more straightforward 'tunes' as such, and his melodies retain the unexpected leaps, chromatic twists and widely-spaced intervals of the piano music, as Ex. 3.5 shows. The way in which the intervals in the vocal line become larger as the phrase progresses in this example is another often-used feature of Berners' vocal writing (see bars 7–8).

Tam - bour bat - tant   et   ventre à   terre J'a- vais quit - té   mon   ré - gi - ment,

Ex. 3.5: 'La fiancée du timbalier', vocal part, bars 7–10

Berners' songs are distinguished from those of his predecessors Debussy and Ravel by his use of much wider intervals in the melodic lines. Where the two French composers favour narrow intervals – mostly up to a perfect fifth, but with a lot of emphasis on monotonal movement, seconds and thirds – Berners frequently uses sixths, sevenths, octaves and ninths. These are occasionally found in Ravel, and later in the songs of André Caplet, but are by no means the norm within the modern French repertoire. Often several such large intervals appear within a single phrase in Berners' songs thereby making zigzag shapes common in the vocal lines. Debussy's and Ravel's melodic lines are frequently suggestive of recitative, whereas Berners' appear as rather more animated speech shapes, whatever language he is setting.

    In addition to the stylistic similarities already noted between the piano music and songs there is also evidence of some direct connections, with the best examples coming from Berners' depictions of laughter. In the previous chapter similarities were noted between figures found in 'Pour une tante à l'héritage' and 'Le rire'. A similar onomatopoeic imitation of a laugh also appears briefly in 'L'étoile filante', in which a light, high titter in the piano anticipates the word 'rire' in bar 3 (see Ex. 3.6). The phrase which follows, 'Dans le soir où je soupire' ('In the evening, when I sigh') is accompanied by three chords which rise and fall much as they did to characterise a sigh in 'Un soupir' from the *Fragments psychologiques* (cf. Ex. 3.7 and Ex. 2.18).

Ex. 3.6: L'étoile filante, bars 2–3

Ex. 3.7: 'L'étoile filante', bars 6–8

Relatively rare in Berners' piano music and songs are passages in which a phrase is repeated several times at the same pitch. There are two notable such passages, however, which are used to considerable effect: in 'The Lady Visitor in the Pauper Ward' from *Three English Songs* at the words 'Leave us to quiet dreaming and slow pain' (Ex. 3.8) and in the solo piano piece *Le poisson d'or* (bar 18 in Ex. 2.2 contains identical material to the preceding three bars). Although not musically similar, both have a hypnotic character – suitably fitting in the contexts in which they appear – which results from the sudden and unexpected use of the repetition of a short motive.

Ex. 3.8: 'The Lady Visitor in the Pauper Ward', bars 15–17

Distinguishing similarities with the piano music in these ways enables us to define Berners' musical style more confidently. But the songs bring another dimension to this too: how he sets words to music, especially considering that he uses texts in three languages. The illustration of particular words in their most literal sense – 'word painting' – occurs most often in the *Lieder Album* and *Trois chansons*, but rarely in the two sets of English songs. In true droll Berners fashion it is used to great effect in 'Du bist wie eine Blume' from the *Lieder Album* to illustrate his claim that the original poem was inspired by the poet's encounter with a white pig rather than a person. From the title, which should be translated into English as 'You are like a flower', but which Berners mischievously 'translates' in parentheses beneath the German as 'The White Pig', it is his aim to 'set the record straight' about what he sees as the hitherto misguided interpretation of the words. As he explains at the head of the score, indubitably with tongue in cheek:

> According to one of Heine's biographers, this poem was inspired by a white pig that the poet had met with in the course of a walk in the country. He was, it appears, for some time afterwards, haunted by the thought of the melancholy fate in store for it and the note of foreboding that runs through the poem is thus explained.
>
> This fact does not seem to have been sufficiently appreciated by those who have hitherto set the poem to music and the present version is an attempt to restore to the words their rightful significance, while at the same time preserving the sentimental character of the German Lied.

The grunts of the pig are heard throughout the piano accompaniment, as shown in Ex. 3.9, and as such serve as a constant reminder of the poem's true and unexpected muse.

Ex. 3.9: 'Du bist wie eine Blume', bars 1–3

There have been many settings of Heine's poem 'Du bist wie eine Blume', notably by Schumann, Schubert, Anton Rubinstein, Liszt and Wolf. Schumann's song is probably the best known, and though Berners' interpretation of the text is entirely different, his phrases often have a Schumannesque shape. The melody at the words 'Ich schau' dich an, und Wehmuth/ Schleicht mir in's Herz hinein' ('As I gaze on thee, foreboding/ Filleth my heart with fear'), for example, is remarkably similar to a phrase from the first song in Schumann's *Dichterliebe* (cf. Ex. 3.10a and b).

Ex. 3.10a: 'Du bist wie eine Blume', bars 12–13

Ex. 3.10b: Schumann, 'Im wunderschönen Monat Mai' from *Dichterliebe*, Op.48, bars 10–12[6]

Berners uses a figure similarly descriptive to his grunting pig at the beginning of the second song from the *Lieder Album*, 'König Wiswamitra'. The opening words, 'The good King Wiswamitra/ Hath lost his Royal head', are given a very literal sense by a graphic illustration in the piano accompaniment of the chopping of an axe. That this sudden leaping figure is heard twice suggests that the initial blow was not successful, and that the executioner has not sharpened his axe properly (see Ex. 3.11). An equally gruesome illustration occurs at the end of 'Theodore, or the Pirate King', the second of the *Three Songs*. Here, in a deliciously affected *sentimentale* passage, the voice, in long held notes, sings 'But Theodore' above rising staccato arpeggios in the piano. The illustrative purpose of these staccato notes becomes clear in the following words 'Though dripping gore'. Such explicit illustrating of the words is frequently a characteristic of a composer's early songs, but also reminds us of Berners' penchant for all things outrageous.

---

[6] Reproduced by kind permission of Peters Edition Limited, London.

Ex. 3.11: 'König Wiswamitra', bars 8–11

Rather more subtle elucidations of the text appear in the *Trois chansons*: a rising four-note figure in the piano accompaniment to 'Romance' suggests the 'flutes' (see Ex. 3.12), whilst low rhythmic interjections imitate the 'drums' described by the singer. In the same song the words, 'Le poids d'une souffrance indue/ Doit s'alléger tôt, bien souvent' ('The weight of unwarranted suffering/ should soon be lightened'), are given a literal meaning by the piano accompaniment. A low and heavy chromatic descent suggests the weight of suffering (Ex. 3.13, bars 10–11), before a higher linking figure in bar 11 looks back to the 'flutes' mentioned earlier and leads to the words 'Doit s'alléger tôt bien souvent'. Here the new-found air of optimism is echoed in the music by the ethereal quality of the accompaniment, in which an unresolved chord of A minor, with an added sharpened 6th (bar 14, Ex. 3.13) is left 'in suspense' by ties.

Ex. 3.12: 'Romance', bar 6

Ex. 3.13: 'Romance', bars 10–14

Berners also uses music to give metaphysical ideas a physical reality in this way at the end of the 'Romance'. The equivocal final words 'After all, the worst is far from certain' inspire an equally ambiguous end to the music, where an anticipated cadence into C major is thwarted by a B major chord with an added ninth in the piano in bar 31 (Ex. 3.14). A suspended G sharp in the voice, though, does not resolve onto an F sharp in bar 31 and continues above the penultimate piano chord. The immaculate voice-leading elsewhere in Ex. 3.14 makes the harmonic surprise at the end doubly effective.

Ex. 3.14: 'Romance', bars 28–32

In the two sets of English songs, Berners concerns himself rather less with word painting, and responds more simply to the moods of the texts. The 'Lullaby' from *Three English Songs*, for example, begins with a gently lilting legato figure in the left hand of the piano beneath a right hand *pianissimo* melody. The supporting harmonics alternate between chords of F minor and E flat major: fluctuating minor – major tonalities are found throughout the song. This opening introduces one of the more 'singable' of Berners' vocal lines (Ex. 3.15), which leads into a sudden key change and a rather more characteristic zigzagging phrase, in which the piano oscillates between chords of E major and G sharp minor. At the words 'Care is heavy therefore sleep you' (Ex. 3.16) the piano accompaniment changes to include a tender, legato rocking figure in the right hand. The simplicity of this 'Lullaby' not only marks it out as Berners' most heartfelt song, but also makes it seem intrinsically English in a way that the two other songs from the set, though effective, do not.

Ex. 3.15: 'Lullaby', bars 5–8

Ex. 3.16: 'Lullaby', bars 20–21

After the relative simplicity of the 'Lullaby' Berners immediately launches into atonality with the second song from the *Three English Songs*, 'The Lady Visitor in the Pauper Ward'. This is the most harmonically obscure of Berners' songs; the first phrase alone employs every note of the chromatic scale[7] (Ex. 3.17). Berners rejects word-painting in favour of reflecting the more general sentiments expressed by Robert Graves' disturbing poem:

> Why do you break upon this old, cool peace,
> This painted peace of ours,
> With harsh dress hissing like a flock of geese,
> With garish flowers?
> Why do you churn smooth waters rough again,
> Selfish old skin-and-bone?
> Leave us to quiet dreaming and slow pain.
> Leave us alone.[8]

Ex. 3.17: 'The Lady Visitor in the Pauper Ward', bars 1–2

Chromaticism abounds, as do awkward leaps in the vocal line (Ex. 3.18). Phrases frequently end with a caesura, preventing the music from flowing smoothly between phrases, and there are sudden changes of tempi and

---

[7] This is not systematic, Berners was not anticipating Schoenberg's 12-note composition method of 1923.

[8] Robert Graves (1895–1985), 'The Lady Visitor in the Pauper Ward' from *Fairies and Fusiliers* (New York, A A Knopf, 1918).

dynamics. In this way, Berners creates a successful musical representation of the torment expressed in the words.

Ex. 3.18: 'The Lady Visitor in the Pauper Ward', vocal part, bars 11–12

The final song in the set derives its title, 'The Green-Eyed Monster', from a play on words. The 'Green-Eyed Monster' refers both to the Dodo of the opening words and to the jealousy of the speaker. Banfield also suggests a hint of music-hall bawdiness in the words:[9]

> James gave Elizabeth a Dodo,
> He only *offered* one to me –
> A lovely lemon-coloured Dodo,
> With the greenest eyes that you could wish to see.[10]

As in the previous song, Berners maintains a strongly chromatic vocal line, which (unlike that in 'The Lady Visitor in the Pauper Ward') is doubled continuously in the top of the right hand piano line. A wonderfully legato passage *poco meno mosso* reflects the sentiments of the speaker as she dreams about the dodo (see Ex. 3.19):

Ex. 3.19: 'The Green-Eyed Monster', bars 5–6

In all three languages Berners' word setting is immaculate, with the stressing being equally natural in each case. His eclecticism is reflected in the fact that he is as much at home setting German and French as he is English, though it is noticeable that of all his songs the most unaffected and natural is the first of the *Three English Songs*, 'Lullaby'. Notably there are

---

[9] Banfield, *Sensibility and English Song*, Volume 2, 1985, 381–82.
[10] Text by Esther Lilian Duff.

far fewer anacruses in the English songs than in the German (only one vocal phrase in the entire *Lieder Album* does not begin with an anacrusis) and this reflects the characteristic intonations of the English and German languages. The settings in French, an unstressed language, contain far more phrases which begin on the second or third beat of the bar than do either the English or German songs, the importance of a strong down-beat on a particular word or syllable being greatly reduced in a less angular language. Despite these differences, the shapes of the vocal lines are strikingly similar in each set, and are characterised by the same wide or awkward leaps, zigzagging movement and chromatic twists. Berners rarely uses melismas in any of his songs, and the few that exist very rarely contain more than two notes on one syllable.

Unfortunately there is no documented evidence as to who first performed these songs, and as there are numerous instances in which the piano accompaniment appears to 'assist' the singer by doubling the vocal line, it might be supposed that Berners expected them to be sung mostly by amateurs. However, though some songs have their vocal line doubled throughout, others contain very little or no such doubling. 'Du bist wie eine Blume', the first song from the *Lieder Album*, for example, contains a very clearly doubled vocal line, whereas the other two songs, 'König Wiswamitra' and 'Weihnachtslied' do not. Another song, 'L'étoile filante' from *Trois chansons*, contains several instances in which the vocal line is doubled by the piano, but this is not consistent throughout. In this particular song there are places where the voice must re-enter, without assistance, after a short piano interlude. In other words, although the singer's note may appear simultaneously in the piano part, the preceding music is not designed to help the singer find it. Occasionally the doubling of the vocal line is interrupted part way through a phrase, but then re-joins; in this way the difficulties for the singer, in terms of accurate pitching, are increased. If Berners did intend the songs to be sung by amateurs he made no concessions; all have considerable technical difficulties for the singer.

Although begun before his piano music, Berners' songs were mostly completed after he had finished writing for solo piano and were a natural progression from that genre at an early stage of his career. Berners' life as a composer spanned a period of thirty-four years and although his musical style did not alter greatly during that time these first songs enabled him to gain experience in word-setting and writing for voices, which was to prove invaluable in his later opera and choral ballet.

Berners was to write his own libretto (in French) for his 1922 opera *Le carrosse du Saint-sacrement*, and was to complete six novels between 1936 and 1942. In view of this it is perhaps surprising that he did not set any of his own texts in these first songs. However, his choice of poems often reveals Berners' personality in a most telling way, and when such perfectly Bernersian wit is found in the poems he set by E L Duff, Robert Graves and John Masefield it is clear that he had no need to write his own.[11] Who else could – or would – have set so sympathetically the lines:

A bloody trade a pirate's trade is.
   But Theodore,
   Though dripping gore,
Was always courteous to the Ladies.[12]

from Masefield's 'Theodore or the Pirate King'? Even in more traditional or serious poems, such as Heine's 'Du bist wie eine Blume', Berners' penchant for the facetious is clearly manifest and helps distinguish his setting from those of his illustrious predecessors. His liking for imitating other styles of writing, first explored in the piano duets and orchestral works *Trois Morceaux* (*Three Pieces for Orchestra*) and *Fantaisie espagnole*, is given another outing in his settings of traditional sea shanties in the *Three Songs* and *Dialogue between Tom Filuter and his man by Ned the dog stealer* in which he parodies the English folk style.

    Taken as a complete set, Berners' songs illustrate that he was a truly cosmopolitan composer who was confident enough and able to display his unique musical personality through his short but often bitingly observant works. Together with his early piano music they showed Berners to be a highly talented musician and helped secure his reputation in influential circles as an important musical figure. Now, though, it was time to try something on a larger scale.

---

[11] It is significant that after his opera Berners was not tempted to set his own text to music again until his c.1940 song 'Red Roses and Red Noses'. In his 1936 choral ballet Berners set text from Gertrude Stein's play *They must. Be wedded. To their wife.* and enlisted the help of Constant Lambert in arranging the words to fit his music, see Chapter 6.

[12] Masefield, *Theodore or the Pirate King*, 1903.

Chapter 4

The Orchestral Music (1917–24)

Although the early part of Berners' career as a composer was largely dominated by small-scale piano music and songs, three short orchestral works also date from that time: *Three Pieces for Orchestra* (1917), *Fantaisie espagnole* (1918–19) and the *Fugue in C minor* (1924). The first two of these were also published as arrangements for piano duet; *Three Pieces for Orchestra* has already been examined (under the title *Trois morceaux*) in Chapter 2. Berners scored this first large-scale piece for a substantially sized orchestra and used its wide palette of tonal colours to great effect straight away. The writing is assured, and Berners does not shy away from adding strands to the texture which were not in the original version for piano duet (following the lead of Debussy and Ravel). To go into detail here about the music of *Three Pieces for Orchestra* would be to restate much of what has been said in Chapter 2, but it is interesting to note that Berners' first orchestral work showed an immediate understanding of how to write for orchestra effectively, and the experience he gained with this piece and with *Fantaisie espagnole* undoubtedly contributed to the direction his musical career was to take from the early 1920s onwards. Evidently buoyed by his successful grasp of the techniques involved in the 1917–19 orchestral works, his output was later dominated by larger-scale pieces: an opera (1920–22) and five ballets (1926–46). He only returned to his previously favoured idiom of piano music very late in his career.

Fantaisie espagnole (1918–19)

Berners' *Fantaisie espagnole* saw him employ the largest body of instruments he would ever use and was therefore a bold step into what was still, to him, a fairly new genre. The instrumentation includes almost quadruple woodwinds, a large brass section, two harps and celeste.[1]

Initially written as a piano solo, begun late in 1918 when he visited Faringdon after inheriting the barony, the three-movement work was orchestrated by Berners in Rome the following June. The piano duet was

---

[1] For the complete instrumentation see Appendix 2.

most likely completed after the orchestration, or simultaneously with it,[2] and was published to enable his work to reach a wider audience than the orchestral version alone; such arrangements of orchestral repertoire were commonplace, and at that time were encouraged by publishers. The complexity of *Fantaisie espagnole*, with several melodic strands often occurring concurrently, suggests that it was unlikely to have been initially conceived as anything other than an orchestral work. The original version for solo piano was never published and was probably just used as the basis for his orchestration.[3] Although the duet is highly effective, the orchestral version seems much more suited to expressing the musical ideas contained within, with varied instrumental timbres being an integral part of the work. Berners' assured handling of a large orchestra owed a debt to early Stravinsky, and the accomplished nature of *Fantaisie espagnole* and *Three Pieces for Orchestra* mirrored the first efforts of Berlioz, Richard Strauss and other renowned orchestrators.

The Romantic ideal, prevalent in much Western music, of celebrating aspects of one's homeland through music with a specifically 'nationalist' flavour affected various Spanish composers of the nineteenth century and the tradition was continued into the twentieth in the music of Albéniz (1860–1909), Granados (1867–1916) and Falla (1876–1946) amongst others. It was nothing new, however, for a non-Spanish composer to find the traditional music of Spain a source of inspiration too. Chabrier's *España* (1883), Rimsky-Korsakov's *Capriccio espagnole* (1887), Ravel's *Rapsodie espagnole* (1907–8) and 'Ibéria' from Debussy's *Images pour orchestre* (1908) demonstrate that Spanish musical idioms fascinated composers of disparate backgrounds. Berners made a particularly successful contribution to the genre with *Fantaisie espagnole* and used the opportunity to prove wrong certain critics who had claimed him incapable of writing a tune. By his own count his Spanish fantasy contained no fewer than seventy.[4] Berners' friend, the composer, conductor and musicologist Constant Lambert was evidently impressed:

It would hardly be an exaggeration to say that the Spanish national style was invented by a Russian, Glinka, and destroyed by an Englishman, Lord Berners; for after the latter's amazingly brilliant parody of Spanish mannerisms it is impossible to hear most Spanish music without a certain satiric feeling breaking through.[5]

---

[2] See Chapter 2.
[3] Berners always composed at the piano.
[4] Amory, 1998, 65.
[5] Constant Lambert, *Music Ho!*, 1934, 171.

Dedicated to the Italian composer and musicologist Gian Francesco
Malipiero (1882–1973), Berners' work was premiered at a Proms concert
on 24 September, 1919, and on 7 June 1921 opened the concert at the
Queen's Hall in which Eugene Goossens conducted the first English
concert performance of Stravinsky's *The Rite of Spring*.

The three contrasting movements of *Fantaisie espagnole* unfold without
a break: a slow and held back 'Prélude' is followed by a much more
aggressively rhythmical 'Fandango', which in turn gives way to a busy
'Pasodoblé' with an unrelenting 'oom-pah' bass. Berners uses similar
devices in each to achieve a Spanish flavour; the influence of traditional
Spanish dance forms and rhythmic devices is clear throughout and
connections with Ravel's four-movement *Rapsodie espagnole* ('Prélude à
la nuit', 'Malagueña', 'Habanera' and 'Feria') are inescapable, especially
when we consider that the 'Malagueña' is a variety of the fandango.

Berners establishes the mood of each movement in the opening bars:
Exx. 4.1–4 show material from the beginnings of the 'Prélude', 'Fandango'
and 'Pasodoblé' which illustrate the differences in character. In all three
movements these introductory motives continue throughout much of what
follows, operating as a steady rhythmic background which supports a
foreground of interweaving melodic themes. In the 'Prélude', for example,
a gentle *dolce* semiquaver motive from the second bar continues through
much of the movement. Berners creates an interesting texture here by using
semi-staccato notes in the clarinet over oscillating legato ones in the muted
violins. Later, this accompanying theme reappears on a low, staccato flute,
simultaneously with a celeste, which plays the same notes, legato, at the
same pitch.[6]

Ex. 4.1: *Fantaisie espagnole*, **'Prélude', piano duet, bars 1–3**

---

[6] The Celeste plays an octave higher than written, so although written in the bass clef this
line sounds at the same pitch as the flute.

The rhythmic impetus in the 'Fandango' is much more driving. Re-iterated quavers in the trumpets and tambourine (Ex. 4.2) are punctuated with accents and sforzandi every half bar. Combined with continuous quick semiquavers (Ex. 4.3) in the bassoons and violas, this creates an urgent, wild atmosphere. Headed *Allegro feroce* the persistent rhythm of these motives propels the 'Fandango' forward, creating an immediate contrast with the gentle 'Prélude'. By the end of the 'Fandango', the half-bar accents have given way to stresses on every quaver as the music surges forward to a fiery conclusion.

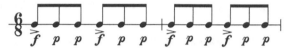

Ex. 4.2: *Fantaisie espagnole*, **'Fandango', tambourine part, bars 1–2**

Ex. 4.3: *Fantaisie espagnole*, **'Fandango', bassoon parts, bars 1–2**

The 'Pasodoblé' begins, *Tempo di Marcia*, at a similar pace to the preceding movement (see Ex. 4.4), although after the densely orchestrated ending of the 'Fandango' the texture is now much thinner. Pizzicato strings pound through a continuous quaver rhythm, providing the pulsating rhythmic drive typical of this dance form. The first and second beats of each bar in 2/4 time are both stressed with accents in the bassoons, giving this movement an immediately energetic, unrelenting feel.

Ex. 4.4, *Fantaisie espagnole*, **'Pasodoblé', piano duet version, bars 1–4**

Throughout *Fantaisie espagnole* Berners' treatment of the orchestra shows an immaculate attention to detail, and a keen awareness of potential problems with balance. Despite the fact that this was only his second such work, his grasp of the intricacies of orchestration suggest that this was a skill he had carefully studied before beginning. How beneficial or enlightening were his orchestration lessons with Edmund Kretschmer is undocumented, and the fact that Berners' music was of a consistently high standard, despite his limited training, even when venturing into complex formal structures (in the *Fugue in C minor*) and into genres hitherto unfamiliar to him, rather points to a combination of devoted self-tuition and a good deal of natural talent.

Berners' approach to orchestral writing led him to treat the wind, brass and string sections equally when allocating background and foreground material. Motives often reappear on different instruments at different pitches across the orchestra, and in this way, despite the fact that repetition is an integral part of the Spanish musical style, Berners avoids letting the work become monotonous. Unlike Rimsky-Korsakov's *Capriccio espagnole* there are no short virtuosic cadenzas for solo players, and the melodic writing for wind instruments is by no means as decorative as that found in Ravel's or Debussy's music. Extended string techniques are restricted to pizzicato and tremolo writing, rather than the sul ponticello or sul tasto effects employed by Debussy. However, *Fantaisie espagnole* is a short work in which Berners' straightforward instrumental writing and clear-cut motives, stem from his preference for directness of expression discussed in previous chapters.

The first movement, 'Prélude', is much less densely orchestrated than the 'Fandango' or 'Pasodoblé'. There is little brass (two horns, and a single trumpet which only plays for two bars), and all melodic motives are played by solo instruments, rather than being doubled. From the opening bars it is clear that the emphasis is on the blending of instrumental timbres, and Berners exploits the instruments' different tonal characteristics by varying the registers in which they play. Ex. 4.5 shows the wind parts from bars 5–9 in which the first melodic themes appear. These simple, short motives often begin with a single note, repeated several times then decorated, and all occur over a continuous tonic pedal note, D, played by the double basses. A mood of restraint and poise contrasts with the following two dance-inspired movements, which give way to wilder, more impassioned emotions.

Ex. 4.5: *Fantaisie espagnole*, 'Prélude', bars 5–9

A meticulous attention to detail in the placing of dynamic markings is further evidence of Berners' ordered approach to orchestral writing. Always making sure that important themes are marked at a higher dynamic level than background themes, Berners leaves nothing to chance. When a melodic line demands a naturally soft register of a particular instrument, such as the low register of the flute, Berners reduces the instrumentation around it to ensure it remains audible. In the 'Pasodoblé' his concern for retaining the desired balance of instruments leads him to give an instruction at the foot of the score, which indicates that if a particular middle register piccolo theme is not heard, the third flute must play in unison with it.[7]

There are several slight differences between the orchestral and piano duet versions of *Fantaisie espagnole* which show that Berners appreciated the differences between what the two mediums could do, and was keen to make the piece as idiomatic as possible for the forces involved. One example concerns a dynamic effect in the third movement. The orchestral score of the 'Pasodoblé' is two bars longer than the piano duet version; at first glance these extra bars seem to be simply an extension of a repeated theme, with a slightly altered harmony, in a loud tutti passage. (See Ex. 4.6, which shows selected instrumental parts from bars 99–102.) However, during these two bars a crescendo is clearly heard in the trombone, the only instrument playing a sustained note. This effect is impossible to create on the piano so Berners omitted these two bars in the duet version of *Fantaisie espagnole*.

---

[7] The third flute part in *Fantaisie espagnole* doubles as a second piccolo where necessary.

Ex. 4.6: *Fantaisie espagnole*, **'Pasodoblé', bars 99–102**

Short crescendos and diminuendos, reminiscent of Ravel, are frequently used to give melodic lines a swirling effect, particularly in the 'Fandango'. The example shown below (Ex. 4.7) is an early flute and trumpet entry in the second movement in which the crescendos and diminuendos for the different instruments are placed at varying points within the bar. As the wind entry dies away the trumpet theme comes to the fore to match the rising and falling shape of the phrase.

Ex. 4.7: *Fantaisie espagnole*, **'Fandango', bars 6–7**

Berners' first orchestral work, *Three Pieces for Orchestra*, had enabled him to demonstrate his skill at imitating the music of other composers and styles, and as such was ideally suited to his talents. *Fantaisie espagnole*, a work inspired by traditional Spanish music, was equally ideal as a subject for an early incursion into orchestral writing because typically such music placed a strong emphasis on short repeated patterns, which mirrored Berners' own compositional style. He captured the spirit of Spain by using particular dance forms, Phrygian mode motives, and rhythmic devices (as shown in Exx. 4.8a–b) that have become synonymous with Spanish culture. It is the incorporation of these time-honoured conceits of Spanish music into *Fantaisie espagnole* that make it one of Berners' most accessible works.

Ex. 4.8a: *Fantaisie espagnole*, 'Pasodoblé', piano score, Primo part, bars 101–102

Ex. 4.8b: *Fantaisie espagnole*, 'Fandango', flute part, bars 70–71

Using traditional dance forms in *Fantaisie espagnole* enabled Berners to draw on established characteristics of the 'Fandango' and 'Pasodoblé' in his music. The fandango, for example, is a passionate courtship dance, in which two dancers provoke and challenge each other with increasingly energetic movements. Castanets, clapping hands, finger clicks and stamping feet punctuate the rhythm and the speed builds up with a gradual *accelerando* to the end. Berners' 'Fandango' contains many of the hallmarks of the traditional dance; a *Più agitato* towards the middle of the movement indicates an increase in tempo, although this is a sudden rather than gradual change, and as the movement progresses energy builds up as more instruments are added to the texture. Accents are used with increasing regularity too, initially to punctuate every half bar, but by the end to stress every quaver. A general pause before the final build up of sound reflects another characteristic feature of the original dance, in which the dancers suddenly stand rigid, the music only resuming when the dancing restarts (Ex. 4.9).

A different version of the fandango is danced by two men as a battle of skill. The first dancer sets the rhythm and steps and is followed by the second who elaborates on these movements. Changing time signatures from 6/8 to 9/8 in Berners' 'Fandango' lengthen particular phrases and give the music an improvisatory quality which is typical of the traditional fandango, but also suggests this idea of elaboration on a set pattern of steps (see Exx. 4.10a and b).

Ex. 4.9: *Fantaisie espagnole*, 'Fandango', piano duet, bars 65–66

Ex. 4.10a: *Fantaisie espagnole*, 'Fandango', oboe parts, bars 3–4

Ex. 4.10b: *Fantaisie espagnole*, 'Fandango', oboe parts, bars 6–7

Despite Berners' use of traditional elements in his Spanish fantasy, the ending of the 'Pasodoblé' shows an acknowledgement of his debt to Stravinsky. As shown in Ex. 4.11 the final bars of *Fantaisie espagnole* bear a remarkable resemblance to those of *The Rite of Spring*. After a *fortissimo* tutti, a brief rest is followed by an ascending scale, heard on a flute, clarinet and harp in Berners' *Fantaisie*, and a flute and alto flute in Stravinsky's *Rite*, before the final chord crashes down. The unmistakable reference is the most clear-cut allusion to Stravinsky in all Berners' music, and it is remarkably coincident that *Fantaisie espagnole* was performed at the concert, mentioned above, in which *The Rite of Spring* received its English concert premiere.

Ex. 4.11: *Fantaisie espagnole*, **'Pasodoblé', bars 170–173**

With *Fantaisie espagnole* completed it was to be another six years before Berners would return to writing for orchestra alone. In the meantime he relinquished his post at the British embassy in Rome and turned his attentions back to the smaller scale medium of song before beginning work on his only opera, *Le carrosse du Saint-sacrement*, which would occupy him until its premiere in 1924.

Fugue in C minor (1924)

In May 1924 Berners was still in Paris after the first performance of the newly revised *Le carrosse du Saint-sacrement* at the Théâtre des Champs-Elysées, and it was then that he wrote his orchestral piece *Fugue in C minor,* which he dedicated to the French patroness of the arts, Princess Edmond de Polignac. Although completed quickly the *Fugue* was not performed until 1926 when it was used as a symphonic interlude between ballet productions at His Majesty's Theatre under the baton of Eugene Goossens. This season also saw the premiere of Berners' first ballet, *The Triumph of Neptune*. The first concert performance of the *Fugue in C minor* was played by the London Symphony Orchestra, conducted by Sir Thomas Beecham, on 7 November 1926 at the Royal Albert Hall, as part of a Sunday afternoon concert series.

It is typically perverse of Berners that after two years spent working on a very modern sounding opera he should then choose to look back to a compositional procedure most popular in the seventeenth century. Whether intended as a parody of an archaic 'academic' style of writing is unclear, although evidence shows that Berners retained a strong interest in such contrapuntal writing later in life. When a nervous breakdown at the start of the Second World War led him to leave London and seek retreat in Oxford, the only music he attempted to write were exercises in counterpoint.[8] Presumably, Berners saw this as an academic activity, one which did not require an emotional response on his part at a time of great emotional upheaval in his life.

Like his opera, Berners' *Fugue in C minor* was an ambitious project for someone whose formal training was, at best, limited. Terrified of being seen as a bore in conversation, it seems that this wariness of monotony affected his musical work too. Berners experimented with new genres throughout his career and set himself challenges in other branches of the arts, which included writing a play and learning to paint; he enjoyed considerable success with both. Several years earlier he had used *Fantaisie espagnole* to prove himself capable of writing a tune in the face of criticism to the contrary; if any commentator had dared suggest Berners would have difficulty with more structurally complex art forms, his *Fugue in C minor* was proof enough that he did not.

Traditionally, fugues were written for between two and eight parts (most often three or four) so by writing an orchestral fugue for a substantial number of instruments Berners was throwing himself in at the deep end of contrapuntal writing.

Berners uses many of the conventional devices from seventeenth-century models in his *Fugue in C minor*. A subject theme in the tonic key is followed by a second appearance in the dominant (the 'answer'); further appearances of the subject, sometimes in inversion, augmentation, with stretto entries, and above pedal points, are interspersed with episodic passages in the traditional manner. These episodes derive much of their thematic material from the subject and increase in length and complexity throughout. Where Berners' fugue deviates from the usual pattern is in the absence of a countersubject: a complementary idea which accompanies the subject and answer themes after the initial statement. The answer in Berners' *Fugue* is accompanied only by staccato quaver chords. To reject a fundamental element of the established fugal procedure in this way was a daring move, not least because the countersubject, in combination with the subject or answer, normally created the contrapuntal texture of the fugue. Instead of achieving counterpoint through the use of a countersubject, Berners used increasingly elaborate material derived from the subject theme beneath its successive appearances. So as the fugue progresses, the contrapuntal writing becomes more complex.

---

[8] Many of these are now held at the British Library.

The long 8-bar subject, which first appears in unison on clarinets, horns and violas, is shown below transposed to concert pitch. It is constructed from several short motives, covers a wide range of notes, and is characterised by sequential movement and chromatic twists.

Ex. 4.12: *Fugue in C minor*, **clarinet part (transposed), bars 1–9**

A sequential figure of a quaver followed by two semiquavers appears in the first two bars, and leads to repeated accented quavers in bar 3. Another sequence of crotchet suspensions, which resolve upwards to the note a semitone above, is used over the next three bars, before an arpeggio leads up to the highest note of the theme, D-flat. From here, a melodic minor scale descends towards the tonic, although the expected key note, C, is avoided when the 'answer' theme begins, instead, on flutes, oboes, clarinets and trombones at the start of bar 9. By using sequences and altering the number of times a motive is repeated Berners was able to vary the length of the subject without altering its overall structure: the first appearance is eight bars long, the second nine, the third seven, and so on.

Berners' use of traditional fugue techniques in his *Fugue in C minor* can be seen in Exx. 4.13–15. Ex. 4.13 shows the subject theme in inversion; although not exact, the overall shape clearly has notes moving in the opposite direction to the subject, as is shown distinctly in Ex. 4.14 in which the two themes are superimposed.

Ex. 4.13: *Fugue in C minor*, **cello part, bars 172–79**

Ex. 4.14: *Fugue in C minor*, **subject theme and inversion**

Towards the end of the *Fugue*, augmented versions of the subject, in which the note values are doubled, appear in stretto across the orchestra. The bassoons, horns, a single trombone and violas begin, and are joined after four bars by a second entry on flutes and violins. The flutes stop after four bars, leaving the theme to be carried on by the violins, with the initial statement continuing underneath. The remaining instruments of the orchestra accompany with material often derived from the subject itself. After another four bars the flutes begin the subject again, now joined by the second violins and oboe. This third entry appears as the initial subject statement draws to a close. Now all the instruments pull together in a series of descending scales before the key changes back to C minor for the final section of the fugue. Here the augmented theme is heard once more in the original key with ornate flourishes in the flutes (see Ex. 4.15) and quick ascending scales in other woodwinds and lower strings. A *rallentando* over the final eight bars lends grandeur to the final *fortissimo* appearance of the subject.

Ex. 4.15: *Fugue in C minor*, **flute part, bars 277–84**

With hindsight it is easy to see how important Berners' orchestral pieces were to his musical career. Not only did they give him experience of writing for a large ensemble, but, crucially, they brought his name to the attention of the concert-going public, and to wider artistic circles. The first performances of the *Three Pieces for Orchestra* and *Fantaisie espagnole* on 8 March and 24 September 1919 directed by renowned conductors at well-known English venues gained Berners important professional recognition. It is doubtful whether Diaghilev would have commissioned him to write for his Ballets Russes in 1926[9] if Berners had had absolutely no experience of orchestral writing, and without *The Triumph of Neptune* the direction of Berners' later career would have been completely different. Berners, of course, did not have the advantage of hindsight, just the

---

[9] See Chapter 6: The Ballets.

encouraging words of composers whom he admired, and a desire to broaden his musical horizons and to achieve parity with his revered French contemporaries. His efforts yielded excellent results; he had proved himself a clear and colourful orchestrator, talented parodist and skilled manipulator of contrapuntal material. The way ahead was clear.

Chapter 5

Le carrosse du Saint-sacrement (1920–22)

The French dramatist Prosper Mérimée (1803–70) completed his rather trivial South American play *Le carrosse du Saint-sacrement* (The Carriage of the Holy Sacrament) in 1828 but its first performances were badly received. Twenty years later, in 1848, a revival fared no better: audiences hissed, and after only six performances the play's run was ended. In 1917, however, the French actress Yvonne Arnaud (1890–1958) staged performances in New York, London and Paris, and this time, at last, the production enjoyed considerable success. It was in Paris that Berners saw the play, and he later commented on the impression it had made upon him:

> I was at once fascinated by the grace, the spirit and the character of this little work...It is true that a piece whose charm lies almost entirely in word and dialogue, where the action, materially speaking, is reduced to the very simplest expression, did not seem to me particularly suitable for musical treatment.[1]

By the time Berners had inherited the barony and given up his job at the embassy in Rome, in June 1919, these initial misgivings must have disappeared. He began turning *Le carrosse du Saint-sacrement* into an opera in 1920, completed it in 1922, but revised it the following year, and it received its first performance on 24 April 1924 at the Théâtre des Champs-Elysées, Paris, in a bill that also included Stravinsky's *L'histoire du soldat* and *La chatte*, a ballet by Henri Sauguet. The score was published by Chester in 1923 and a revised edition appeared in 1926.

The action in this one-act, eight-scene opera takes place in the office of the Viceroy of Peru sometime during the eighteenth century. The Viceroy must choose between going to an important church service, attended by all the local dignitaries, or remaining at his official residence to attend to affairs of the state. Eager to show off his new carriage he decides that travelling to the service is a far more enticing option. Unfortunately,

---

[1] Amory, 1998, 85.

though, he has gout (which he insists is merely tiredness) and when he tries to stand, the pain in his leg is overwhelming; he must stay indoors after all.

His private secretary, Martinez, lists some of the more pressing matters requiring the Viceroy's attention, but the Viceroy prefers to gossip, and questions Martinez about La Périchole, a notorious actress and mistress to the Viceroy (among others). After much prompting, Martinez repeats the local speculation that La Périchole is having an affair with the famous matador Ramon. The Viceroy is furious with Martinez, whom he accuses of lying, and demands that he leave at once.

La Périchole turns up at the Viceroy's office with a favour to ask of him. She wants to borrow his new carriage to travel to the service. Although he concedes (out of La Périchole's earshot) that the favour is trifling, the Viceroy decides to question her about her relationship with Ramon before he will deign to consider her request. Indignant, she refutes his allegations about her supposed affair, and oblivious to her obvious guilt he begs for forgiveness, giving her his new carriage by way of apology. La Périchole accepts the gift and heads off at once for the service.

Through a telescope the Viceroy tracks her journey to the church. He watches as her carriage goes too fast and crashes into another, which overturns. In the ensuing uproar Ramon comes to the aid of La Périchole, who then continues her journey at high speed, almost driving through the front door of the church, interrupting the service and causing yet more scandal.

After the service La Périchole returns to the Viceroy's office, accompanied, to everyone's great surprise, by the Bishop of Lima. After a 'revelation' by the Virgin Mary she has decided to donate the carriage to the church in order that the Holy Sacrament might be delivered to the dying rather more quickly than previously possible, thus helping to save more souls from damnation. This final, happy conclusion leaves the Bishop overwhelmed, the Viceroy pleased (miraculously his gout disappears) and La Périchole relieved to be assured of eternal life, thanks to her charitable gesture.

Berners provided the libretto for the opera himself, taking dialogue largely from the second half of Mérimée's play. *Le carrosse du Saint-sacrement* seems to have appealed to him because of its farcical situations, humorous exchanges between characters, and tongue-in-cheek slant on religion, all elements to which Berners was particularly drawn. Unlike his later ballets *Luna Park* (1930) and *A Wedding Bouquet* (1936), which are similarly comic, there is no element of come-uppance for the foolish protagonists, and at the end, incredibly, everyone is content.[2]

Although this is a comic opera,[3] the focus for the humour and the tool with which the situations are unravelled is the dialogue (which is all sung) rather than the on-stage action, as Berners conceded in his comments above. The entire opera is set in the Viceroy's office and the simplicity of the setting contrasts markedly with the Wagnerian scenery he used to recreate in dolls' houses to entertain his family with enactments of grand-scale operas.[4] The active role he took in designing the stage settings and costumes for his later ballet *A Wedding Bouquet*, though, indicates that a strong interest in the visual element of a musical stage work remained, despite the sparseness of the setting for *Le carrosse du Saint-sacrement*.[5]

By the time Berners began work on his opera he had completed only a limited number of other serious works, of which the majority were small-scale piano solos and songs. An opera, therefore, was a serious undertaking and highly ambitious project, but was a challenge Berners rose to and met admirably. Written early in his career when his musical language was at its most obscure, *Le carrosse du Saint-sacrement* is not immediately as accessible a work as *The Triumph of Neptune* and *Luna Park* would later prove to be. However, it was a very important achievement for a composer of Berners' limited orchestral experience and gave him the confidence and experience to embark on the ballets which brought him widespread acclaim.

The eight scenes in *Le carrosse du Saint-sacrement* follow on from each other without a break, and the entire opera lasts only about seventy

---

[2] Translations of the libretto into German and English have been completed by the important German music critic Oskar Bie, and Adam Pollock respectively. A copy of the former, translated as *Die sakramentskutsche* is held at the British Library. The English translation was provided for a performance of the opera recorded in 1983 by the BBC to mark the centenary of Berners' birth. This recording was released on CD in 2000 (Marco Polo 8.225155).

[3] Although *Le carrosse du Saint-sacrement* is a comic opera with a French libretto, it is not an 'opéra comique'. If it is necessary to locate a stylistic model for Berners' work, more similarities are found with Italian opera buffa, which were sung throughout, than the French equivalent which included passages of spoken dialogue not found in *Le carrosse du Saint-sacrement*.

[4] Recounted in *A Distant Prospect*, 1945, Chapter XI 'Bayreuth at Home'.

[5] See Chapter 6: The Ballets.

minutes.[6] Berners rejected the established idea of beginning with the orchestra, commenting:

> Although this is a comic opera, or if you prefer it, a *comédie musicale*, I have laid aside the traditional overture or prelude, the utility of which I fail to see… As regards style you will see that I have not adhered to the old tradition of different airs and scenes following each other, and bound together by the different turns of the intrigue: Mérimée's comedy unfolds itself in too continuous and concise a manner not to induce me to follow its line by a musical development that is held together in the style of a symphonic poem.[7]

In fact, Berners dispenses with any introduction to the action, beginning straight away with singer and orchestra together (see Ex. 5.1). By referring to the work as similar stylistically to a symphonic poem, Berners indicates that there is a single-movement span to the opera. However, despite the length of the work, his preference for variation over development of musical material is clear throughout. Within each scene he tends to divide the music into relatively short sections, often using and repeating certain themes for a particular passage of dialogue between two characters, and moving on to new material when the subject changes or a new character appears. This new material usually begins afresh, often with a change of tempo and time signature, rather than emerging or developing from the preceding music. In this way long scenes are divided up into more 'manageable' chunks. Considering Berners' lack of experience with large-scale forms it is unsurprising that he chose to work in this Satiean way.

Ex. 5.1 shows the opening of the opera. In this initial exchange between Martinez and the Viceroy there are two important themes from which the ten-bar extract is constructed. The first is shown bracketed as 'A'. This three-note figure opens the first scene and is heard in unison in the voice and orchestra. Martinez's initial phrase ends with a descending figure (bracketed as 'B') which is transposed and extended in a bass motive heard in bars 3–4 ('B¹'). Further instances of the 'A' and 'B' motives are shown on the score below. Notably these themes appear in the orchestral *and* vocal lines: despite the importance of the dialogue the voice parts are not set apart from the orchestra here, but are constructed from the same musical material.

---

[6] The original version would have been slightly longer; in the revised edition of 1926 several short passages were cut or rewritten.

[7] Amory, 1998, 85.

Ex. 5.1: Scene 1: bars 1–10

This technique of using short motives as the basis for the construction of a larger section of music occurs throughout *Le carrosse du Saint-sacrement*. After the extract shown above, for example, Berners introduces new themes which are used in the same way over the next thirty bars but which are unrelated thematically to the opening material. Although the overall effect is one of through-composition, Berners clearly preferred to work with small-scale structures even within a large-scale work, and this continued to be the case later in his career when he turned his attention to ballet.

As mentioned above, repeated motives in the orchestral parts of *Le carrosse du Saint-sacrement* often continue under a particular passage of dialogue between two characters and move onto other musical material when the conversation changes or another character appears. The dialogue itself is rapidly enunciated and is frequently set in a semi-parlando style: vocal lines are often constructed to imitate the inflections of natural speech rather than being designed for their particular melodic characteristics. As in Berners' early songs, again as with Satie, instances of melisma are rare;[8] the sheer quantity of text means that there is little time for dwelling on particular words. The vocal lines also contain large intervals: 6ths and 7ths appear quite often and leaps of over an octave are used particularly when a character is expressing anger; the term 'raising one's voice' is hereby given a literal meaning in pitch terms as well as being reflected through increased dynamic levels. Such wide leaps and lack of melismas are also a feature of Berners' early songs, which date from around the same time as *Le carrosse du Saint-sacrement* and are discussed in Chapter 3.

Occasionally Berners refers back to a motive he used in a previous scene in order to highlight a particular reference made in the text, or to suggest a connection that has not been overtly made onstage. In Scene 1, for example, after Martinez tells the Viceroy that he must decide for himself whether or not to go to the service in Lima, an *incisivo* gesture (a variant of 'B' shown in Ex. 5.2) suggests that the Viceroy suddenly makes up his mind: he will go. With the decision made, he and Martinez go on to imagine the effect that the sight of the new carriage will have on the people of Lima, and the motive now assumes a gleeful character. Used in sequence above a staccato bassline (Ex. 5.3) it builds up in a long crescendo as the pair become more and more carried away.

Ex. 5.2: Scene 1, bars 42–43

---

[8] In the original version (before cuts were made for the revised edition of 1926) there are only 52 instances of melisma in the entire opera; of these, 49 are simple two-notes-per-syllable slurs, and the remaining three contain three notes.

Ex. 5.3: Scene 1, bars 66–69

There is a noticeable similarity here with the 'Fate' theme from Bizet's *Carmen* (1875). Ex. 5.4a shows the first appearance of this theme in the Prelude to Act I of Bizet's opera, Ex. 5.4b a later iteration when Carmen first appears onstage. Theme 'B' in Ex. 5.1, like Bizet's motive, uses the first four notes of the descending harmonic minor scale, but Berners distorts the intervals in Exx. 5.2, 5.3 and 5.5 whilst copying the shape of Bizet's phrase. (The similarities between the plots of the two operas – both based on stories by Prosper Mérimée – are also marked: though one is a tragedy and the other light-hearted, both concern a love triangle: a jealous lover, a bullfighter and a rather tempestuous heroine. The ending of *Le carrosse du Saint-sacrement* shows unanticipated harmony between the characters; unanticipated harmony *in musical terms* in the final bars of a piece is one of Berners' compositional trademarks.)

Ex. 5.4a: Bizet, *Carmen*, Prelude to Act I, 'Fate' theme

Ex. 5.4b: Bizet, *Carmen*, Act I, 'Fate' theme

In Scene 5 the Viceroy realises that he cannot go to the service after all because the pain in his leg is too great, and immediately after he tells Balthasar that he has no regrets about not being able to go, the theme reappears. Shown in Ex. 5.5 this brief iteration acts as a poignant reminder of the fun the Viceroy was anticipating, but will now miss. Despite his attempts to 'put on a brave face' it is clear that he truly wanted to go, and the fact that the gout in his leg is preventing him is evidently a cause of great remorse.

Ex. 5.5: Scene 2, bars 85–87

The technique of repeating short motives is also employed occasionally in the vocal parts of the opera, when one character wishes to mimic another. An example of this is shown below in Ex. 5.6. In this passage, from Scene 4, the Viceroy clearly wants to turn the subject of his conversation with La Périchole back to her alleged affair after she has cunningly managed to digress. The actress teasingly copies the Viceroy's voice at his words 'En fait d'amants...' (translated in the English libretto as 'As for your lovers...'). His subtle attempt to steer the topic of discussion back to her supposed indiscretion with the matador has clearly not escaped La Périchole's notice, and her repetition of the Viceroy's motive here lets him know that she's aware of what he is trying to do.

Ex. 5.6: Scene 4, bars 199–202

Ex. 5.7: Scene 3, bar 701

The four-note motif used here actually first appeared in the previous scene when Martinez was recounting the local gossip about La Périchole's behaviour at a bullfight in which Ramon was taking part. In the extract shown in Ex. 5.7 he imitates La Périchole's cry to the matador as he killed the bull. With Martinez's words still ringing in his ears, the Viceroy's use of this motif in the passage shown above in Ex. 5.7 leaves us in no doubt about to whom he is referring in the term 'd'amants'.

Another example of this kind of imitation is shown below in Ex. 5.8. Here, later in Scene 4, the Viceroy tells La Périchole that he knows she would rather be with Ramon than with him. La Périchole copies the Viceroy's pronunciation of 'Ramon', and the Viceroy in turn copies her words and melody when she provokingly admits to having just seen the matador. It is evidently La Périchole's intention to 'wind up' the Viceroy and he naively rises to the bait.

Ex. 5.8: Scene 4, bars 105–115

This kind of imitation adds to the humour of the dialogue, and when themes reappear in different scenes of the opera – either in the vocal or orchestral parts – the music is able to indicate that although a character says one thing, he or she may well be thinking something quite different. In a way unique to music, the listener is able to infer something which has not been made explicit, and another dimension is added to the on-stage action.

Chapter 1 discussed Berners' character, referring to his penchant for shocking people with extravagant practical jokes or eccentric behaviour, and it is notable that he was equally as fond of putting surprises into his scores as he was of startling guests at his homes. There are some typically perverse, though subtle, touches in Berners' score of *Le carrosse du Saint-sacrement*. At the end of the first scene, for example, mention of the Bishop is marked by a sudden change in the orchestral writing from staccato quaver movement to long sustained 'religioso' chords which are much simpler harmonically than the previous music. Ex. 5.9 shows how C major (bar 72), A minor and E minor (bar 73) triads in this section are only 'disturbed' in the following bar by the appearance of a B-flat in the C major triad. Ostensibly this creates a simple unresolved seventh chord, but the interval of a tritone (the 'devil in music') between the B-flat and E at the mention of 'la chaire' ('the pulpit'), along with flippant grace notes in bar 74, has the hallmarks of a typically contrary Bernersian swipe at organised religion.

Ex. 5.9: Scene 1, bars 72–78

Another indication of Berners' 'contrariwise' character is revealed through his use of a particular recurring motif. The leading characters in *Le carrosse du Saint-sacrement* do not have individual musical themes, in the form of a leitmotif, to indicate their presence on stage, but the servant, Balthasar (the Viceroy's valet), does. The theme, shown below in Ex. 5.10, is initially heard at the beginning of the second scene when Balthasar appears on stage for the first time, and is repeated later in the scene as he helps the Viceroy to his feet. It is heard at the end of the third scene when Balthasar shows La Périchole into the study, and further repetitions are heard during the fourth scene when he is twice summoned by the Viceroy. Balthasar speaks briefly in Scene 5 (in which the Viceroy watches La Périchole's disastrous carriage journey) but his theme is not heard. Notably, however, the theme has previously most often been heard when Balthasar enters or exits the stage; in Scene 5 he is present on-stage from the beginning though does not speak until towards the end. Neither does his theme occur at the end of Scene 7 when Balthasar dashes on stage to announce the Bishop's arrival with La Périchole. Use of the motive, therefore, is not systematic but is clearly intended to be associated with the character; the theme does not appear every time Balthasar speaks, but every time it is repeated Balthasar is present. Interestingly Scene 6 – a short orchestral entr'acte with only a few words from the Viceroy and Balthasar – originally[9] contained a fair amount of dialogue and no iteration of Balthasar's theme. However, for the 1926 edition Berners cut thirty bars of a monologue given by the Viceroy and replaced it with a longer orchestral section, making Balthasar now the first character to speak in this scene. Before his words Berners now lets Balthasar's theme ring out clearly in the upper woodwind. Ex. 5.11 shows an iteration of the theme from Scene 4.

Ex. 5.10: Scene 2, bars 1–8

Ex. 5.11: Scene 4, bars 1107–1111

Berners' claim, cited above, to have eschewed the idea of conventional number opera in which 'different airs and scenes [follow] each other', does not give an entirely accurate impression of his work. Although the opera is in one act, with its various scenes uninterrupted by breaks, the style of writing frequently shifts between recitative-like passages, with sustained chords in the orchestral parts beneath static vocal writing, passages of more animated dialogue between characters, and aria-like sections for individual protagonists. These latter passages often occur after a character announces

---

[9] In the 1923 edition.

that he or she has something to say, such as the Viceroy's comment in Scene 3 'Eh bien, Martinez, apprends ce qui me tracasse' ('Listen Martinez, this is what's worrying me'). A change of tempo and instrumentation and an orchestral introduction then 'set the scene' before the character begins his tale. There is little conventional about these aria-like sections; they are through-composed, not particularly 'melodic' and do not end with a clear cadence but rather merge back into recitative or other dialogue. The most obvious change is not in the vocal writing but in the orchestral parts beneath, which tend to take on a rather more prominent role than at other times. This fusion of recitative and aria creates a continuously unfolding drama and was a feature of eighteenth century Italian opera buffa. Unlike the French opéra comique, in which the music was interspersed with passages of spoken dialogue, these were sung throughout, and the words were mainly set syllabically as they are in Berners' *Le carrosse du Saint-sacrement*. By borrowing ideas from earlier models and using them in his own unique way, Berners took a neo-classical approach to writing his only opera. Importantly, despite the uninterrupted nature of the action, Berners continued to use small-scale structures within the frame of a large-scale work, a mode of working which best suited his talents and experience.

Berners' confidence in handling the orchestra allowed him to use it in a variety of ways which range from remaining completely silent beneath a vocal line, to occupying almost an entire scene (Scene 6) without vocal intrusion. When La Périchole makes her first appearance, in Scene 4, the orchestra remains silent through much of her angry confrontation of the Viceroy. Her words are as clear as her mood is bad, and the orchestra's 'stunned' silence heightens the impact of her tirade. Later in the scene, references to Spain, to where the Viceroy threatens to send La Périchole, give rise to the appearance of Spanish musical effects in the orchestral writing, and show Berners using the orchestra to highlight something a character has said. Similarly, mention of the bishop in Scene 1 gave rise to the 'religioso' sustained chords shown above in Ex. 5.9. These return as the bishop speaks in Scene 8, but now 'celestial' rising arpeggios on the harp are heard first as he appears with La Périchole at the Viceroy's study, and later at mention of the Virgin Mary, and show Berners using clichéd musical devices to comic effect. It was the humour of the original play which had drawn Berners to *Le carrosse du Saint-sacrement,* and he took every opportunity to enhance the comedy of the dialogue through the music.

****

Reactions against the excesses of the late Romantics took twentieth century opera in many different directions. Subject matter became much more varied than it had previously been and in many cases the traditional hierarchical tonal system was replaced by the more egalitarian methods of atonality or twelve-tone serialism. There seemed to be as many different approaches to operatic form as there were musical movements. Diverse ideas and styles were explored, from symbolism (Debussy's *Pelléas et Melisande*, 1902), twelve-tone serialism (Berg's *Wozzeck*, 1925), neo-classicism (Stravinsky's *Pulcinella*, 1920, Hindemith's *Cardillac*, 1926), nationalism in the works of Janáček, Bartók, Prokofiev and others, to minimalism in the operas of Philip Glass and John Adams.

New comic operas during the twentieth century were relatively rare. The niche that they had once filled in the popular market had been largely taken over by the operettas of Léhár (1870–1948) and Romberg (1887–1951) amongst others. The musicals of, for example, Kern, Gershwin and Cole Porter were also capturing the imaginations of audiences whose taste for high-brow art was beginning to wane. Ravel completed a comic opera *L'Heure espagnole* in 1907 which was produced in Paris to a mixed reception in 1911, and later Poulenc would follow suit with *Les mamelles de Tirésias* (1940–44) and Britten with *Albert Herring* (1947). But *Le carrosse du Saint-sacrement* was essentially one of a declining breed. The fact that comic opera had evidently lost much of its former popularity is another likely reason why Berners did not venture back into the genre.

Berners' contribution to the operatic repertoire is a curious mixture. Set in the eighteenth century and yet utterly modern in sound, it has an orchestration after Offenbach – far removed from the indulgences of the late nineteenth century – yet is in a form likened by Berners to a symphonic poem, a title devised by Liszt for a format far more popular in the nineteenth century than the twentieth.

After the premiere of *Le carrosse du Saint-sacrement* Berners went back to the medium of orchestral music for a single work, *Fugue in C minor*, before returning to the musical stage in 1926 with *The Triumph of Neptune*, the first of the five ballets which were to dominate his career from then on. The opera was never staged in England; perhaps it was thought that the importance of the dialogue and the rapidity with which the words are sung meant that a production in French in a non-French-speaking country was unlikely to be a great success. Perhaps too, Berners did not want to take on the task of translating the libretto into English; by 1924 he had already spent four years working on the music. Curiously, the British press were rather more generous in their praise for the production than their French counterparts, but the successful introduction to the musical stage that Berners had hoped for had been something of a let down, and, afraid that his work on *Le carrosse du Saint-sacrement* had been a waste of time, he and Constant Lambert arranged some of the orchestral interlude music into another short orchestral work, *Caprice péruvien*. Opera was not a medium to which Berners returned; he had set himself a challenge and had overcome it admirably, but the future of his musical career was to lie elsewhere.

Chapter 6

The Ballets (1926–46)

In the first volume of his autobiography Berners tells how it was the visual impact of the score rather than the sound itself which first attracted him to music.[1] Considering this, it is perhaps not surprising that ballet – a medium which places a strong emphasis on the appearance of the stage, sets and costumes – was to exert a particular fascination. Between 1926 and 1946 he completed five ballets:[2] *The Triumph of Neptune* (1926), *Luna Park* (1930), *A Wedding Bouquet* (1936), *Cupid and Psyche* (1938–9), and *Les Sirènes* (1946). Of these the first three were by far the most successful and enjoyed much greater critical acclaim than the latter two productions.

Ballet was the perfect medium for Berners: it suited his musical style which favoured the colourful and characteristic cameo. There was no need for lengthy development sections which, like Debussy and Satie, he chose to reject. Moreover, as a socialite with a strong interest in literature and painting, ballet gave him the opportunity to socialise and collaborate with like-minded artists while simultaneously creating a work of art. Berners' lifelong interest in ballet brought him in contact with some of the major names in contemporary choreography, literature and art: Serge Diaghilev, Frederick Ashton, Georges Balanchine, Gertrude Stein, Sacheverell Sitwell and Christopher Wood amongst others.

Although Berners frequently returned to the medium of ballet, he completed only a single opera, *Le carrosse du Saint-sacrement* (1920–2), discussed in Chapter 5. Opera should have been another ideal medium for him because, like ballet, long development sections were not obligatory, and the opportunities for collaborations abounded. But Berners spent two

---

[1] 'Both in the earliest developments of my individual taste, as also in later life, the visual sense has always predominated. Even to music I was at first attracted by its graphic symbolisation. The aural side of music held, at first, no charms for me' (Berners, *First Childhood*, 1934, 56).

[2] Amory suggests that a sixth ballet, *Waterloo and Crimea*, was performed in 1933 at the Lyric Hammersmith (1998, 116), but it is likely that this was a short reworking of some of the music from *The Triumph of Neptune* and was one of two such ballets; the other was titled *Le Boxing*. Such adaptations were common among ballet circles; the music from Berners' 1930 ballet *Luna Park* was used by Frederick Ashton for his 1932 production *Foyer de danse* to an entirely different scenario. Ashton was later to work on the choreography for *A Wedding Bouquet*, *Cupid and Psyche* and *Les Sirènes*.

years writing his opera, and a further two years revising it and preparing it for performance; although it was fairly well received it is likely that the process had simply been too protracted, and sufficient to disenchant a composer who had hitherto produced only short works. Notably, whereas Berners had completed his own libretto for *Le carrosse du Saint-sacrement* (based on Prosper Mérimée's play of the same title), he enlisted the help of Constant Lambert in setting Gertrude Stein's words to music in his later choral ballet *A Wedding Bouquet*. This would seem to suggest that word setting in an extended piece was not Berners' favourite activity and might help to explain why he did not return to the operatic stage.

The Triumph of Neptune (1926)

Despite its international acclaim, the Ballets Russes was a private enterprise which relied on private funding to survive. Throughout Diaghilev's management and administration of the company (1909–29) the necessity of finding patrons who were adequately rich and sufficiently interested in ballet to sponsor new productions remained an on-going problem.

Early in 1926 the company's need for financial assistance came to the attention of the London newspaper magnate Lord Rothermere,[3] who had first met Diaghilev two years earlier. In March 1926 they received his first pledge of a two thousand pounds guarantee to underwrite the next summer's independent London season. This season ran between 14 June and 23 July of that year, and included the first performances in England of four ballets: Stravinsky's *Les noces*, Constant Lambert's *Romeo and Juliet*, Auric's *La pastorale* and Satie's *Jack-in-the-Box*.[4] According to Serge Grigoriev, Diaghilev's producer/production manager, Rothermere's assistance ensured a successful season for the company, and the loan was quickly repaid. Rothermere immediately offered further support, in return for which he requested that an English work[5] be included in the programme

---

[3] 1868–1940.

[4] All four of these ballets had been premiered abroad: *Les noces* in Paris on 13 July 1923, *Romeo and Juliet* in Monte Carlo on 4 May 1926, *La pastorale* in Paris on 29 May 1926 and *Jack-in-the-Box* also in Paris on 3 June 1926. Lord Rothermere's support for the 1926 season applied only to the London productions, and in order to finance performances in Monte Carlo Diaghilev sold the curtain Picasso had made for *Le tricorne* along with some figure-paintings Picasso had created for *Cuadro Flamenco* (Grigoriev, 1953, 218–19).

[5] 'At the express wish of Diaghilev's backer, Lord Rothermere, [the new ballet] was to be very English in every way' (Macdonald, 1975, 339).

for the following season.[6] This season ran from 13 November to 11 December 1926, being for the first time at the Lyceum, rather than His Majesty's Theatre. The following year *The Triumph of Neptune* was taken to Monte Carlo, and later productions were also staged in Antwerp and Paris. The ballet was guaranteed a wider audience when a suite, using nine numbers[7] (almost half the music) from the original score was arranged for performance in the concert hall. Championed by Sir Thomas Beecham, two early recordings were made by him, in 1937 with the London Philharmonic Orchestra and in 1952 with the Philadelphia Orchestra, making *The Triumph of Neptune* Berners' most widely recognised music.

Rothermere's request for a quintessentially English ballet was that of an astute modern businessman: with his eye on the profit margins, he aimed to present a crowd-pleasing production which would appeal to the London audiences of the day. He also urged Diaghilev to ensure tickets for the entire season remained low-priced,[8] indicating that the objective was to attract as large an audience as possible, so as to guarantee the recovery of his initial layout. Over the course of the season the company presented a programme of twenty ballets, four of which had not been seen before in London. *The Triumph of Neptune*, as an entirely new production, was only ready late on, and although the premiere on 3 December 1926 was well received, its run ended on 11 December. Nevertheless the whole season was an undisputed success, described by one of those involved as 'one of the most brilliant…we ever had'.[9]

The Ballets Russes' need to produce a new English ballet proved fortuitous for Berners. Having been acquainted with Diaghilev since 1916, he went to see the impresario in July 1926 (presumably unaware of Rothermere's request) to show him a few compositions he thought might be suitable for a ballet. Diaghilev, conscious of his backer's stipulation, agreed and *The Triumph of Neptune* was commissioned. Throughout his career Diaghilev was to commission only two scores from English composers, the other being Constant Lambert's *Romeo and Juliet* (1924–5). It is perhaps surprising, therefore, that Diaghilev chose Berners, who until then had only produced one stage work, his opera *Le carrosse du Saint-sacrement*. Berners, however, was a renowned figure in British public life, and it is

---

[6] Grigoriev, 1953, 224–5.

[7] The order of the numbers was completely changed. See Appendix 2.

[8] Garafola, 1989, 252. According to Nesta Macdonald in *Diaghilev observed by critics in England and the United States 1911–1929*, 1975, 339, the top-priced tickets were 17/-, the front rows of the gallery bookable at 2/4, and the unreserved seats 2/- and 1/-.

[9] Grigoriev, 1953, 223.

likely that Diaghilev's commissioning had more to do with the desire to attract a curious press and London public to his productions, than of his being impressed with Berners' writing. Diaghilev, too, would have been well aware of Berners' elevated financial status, and though there is no evidence to suggest that Berners needed to subsidise the production, he would have been well placed to do so if required. This is not to detract from the quality of Berners' completed score,[10] but the act of commissioning music for a ballet from a novice in the field was a daring move for someone in Diaghilev's financial position.

The next stage was to find a scenario for the ballet and for this Diaghilev turned to Sacheverell Sitwell. Unable to find a suitable literary idea, Sitwell took Diaghilev to see the work of Benjamin Pollock and H J Webb, who designed 'penny plain and twopence coloured' set designs for children's model theatres. Diaghilev bought several of these Victorian prints which supplied the idea for sets and costumes, and inspired by these Sitwell devised the outline of his pantomime ballet. His plan comprised twelve individual scenes – or tableaux – which were 'so entirely disconnected that any one of them might be omitted – as some of them subsequently were (the ballet being found to be far too long) – without injury to the rest'.[11]

A magic telescope on London Bridge points to Fairyland, which a journalist and a gallant sailor, Tom Tug, resolve to explore. After a Classical Interlude, 'Cloudland', in which two Sylphs dance, the adventurers set off on a bus, and, as they leave, a Dandy begins to seduce Tug's wife. The explorers are shipwrecked and saved by a Goddess, Britannia, whilst in Fleet Street rival newspapers, 'The Evening Telescope' and 'The Evening Microscope', compete for news of the expedition. In Fairyland the Fairy Queen watches fairies dance in the Frozen Forest. The Dandy and Tug's wife dance a polka but are interrupted by a drunk singing 'The Last Rose of Summer'. They seek refuge in a house where their shadows appear on a blind and are joined by that of Tom Tug, knife poised, ready to defend his honour. Two policemen go to intervene but as they try to grasp Tug he vanishes and returns to Cloudland.

---

[10] The score is dedicated 'To Viscount Rothermere. London. December, 1926'.

[11] Grigoriev, 1953, 226.

Back on London Bridge a drunken black man, Snowball, upsets the telescope, destroying all connections with Fairyland. Tug becomes the Fairy Prince and marries Neptune's daughter.

The orchestral works Berners completed between 1918 and 1924 had given him plenty of experience in writing for a large number of instruments, and as a result he was confident enough to score this first ballet for one of the largest orchestras he would ever use. This is the liveliest of Berners' ballet scores and the orchestral effects – especially from the percussion – are often as fantastical as the pantomime plot. (The full orchestration for each ballet[12] appears in the list of works in Appendix 2).

Rothermere's request that the new ballet should be intrinsically English was partially satisfied by the pantomime theme, but Berners also attempted to make the music *sound* English in certain scenes through the imitation of the 'pastoral' style of many of his English contemporaries. One example, which shows the opening of the second scene 'Cloudland', is given in Ex. 6.1: the example shows a piano reduction, but in the orchestrated version strings provide the underlying texture here whilst around it a solo oboe and horn weave snatches of melody and countermelody. The 'Englishness' arises from the string background, use of consecutive octaves and a modal melody which creates the 'vague sense of something folkish' noted by Goddard in his comments on Vaughan Williams' *The Lark Ascending* (1914).[13] With this, Berners proved himself capable of affectionate pastiche of an English modal musical style which was dissimilar to his own just as effectively as he had suggested Spanish styles in his earlier *Fantaisie espagnole* (1918– 19), Russian in 'Kasatchok' and Chinese in 'Chinoiserie' from the *Trois Morceaux*.

Ex. 6.1: *The Triumph of Neptune,* **piano reduction, 'Cloudland', bars 1–8**

---

[12] Excepting *Cupid and Psyche.*
[13] Goddard, Scott: 'Ralph Vaughan Williams, O.M.' from *British Music of Our Time,* ed. Bacharach, A L, 1946, 88.

Berners' use of pastiche in *The Triumph of Neptune* extends beyond English styles: in the Scene I 'Schottische' his inspiration is evidently Scottish folk music. The example below (Ex. 6.2) shows a piano reduction of a passage from this scene in which a traditional-sounding Scottish reel rings out in the wind and brass over a droning pedal G-natural in the strings. Notably, though, he astutely avoids the 'Scottish snap' throughout this scene.

Ex. 6.2: *The Triumph of Neptune*, **piano reduction, 'Schottische', bars 67–68**

Despite the overtly British elements in the music of *The Triumph of Neptune*, the true cosmopolitan nature of Berners' compositional style is frequently evident. A waltz in the second scene reminds us of his earlier piano work *Valses bourgeoises* (1917)[14] and the appearance of seventh chords here (Ex. 6.3, bars 78-79) attests to the influence of Ravel on his work.

Ex. 6.3: *The Triumph of Neptune*, **piano reduction, 'Cloudland', bars 76–79**

The variety in character of the different sections of the score led Lane to describe it 'as diverse as it is continually inventive',[15] and in addition to the

---

[14] The waltz was a favoured dance form for Berners; in addition to the work mentioned above, the second of the *Trois morceaux* (1919) is a 'Valse sentimentale', a waltz also appears towards the end of *A Wedding Bouquet* (1936), and he completed a Chopinesque *Valse* for solo piano in 1943, which was also used in the film *The Halfway House*.

[15] CD liner notes to *Lord Berners: The Triumph of Neptune, L'Uomo dai baffi, Valses bourgeoises, Polka*, Marco Polo 8.223711, recorded 1996, issued 1998, 6.

stylistic changes within and between scenes Berners frequently alters the size of the orchestra to reflect what is happening on stage. The end of the 'Entry of Neptune's chariot' in the ninth scene, for example, uses a very full orchestra to reflect the magnificence of the occasion, whereas by way of contrast the following 'Dance of the Fairy Princess' is more lightly scored to suggest her modest refinement.

Berners himself described his music for *The Triumph of Neptune*: 'variegated as a Christmas tree. You will find a little of everything in it from Tchaikovsky to Léo Delibes. And above all it is not in the least "modern"'.[16] The music is unquestionably accessible – this accounts for its immediate popularity – but by claiming to avoid modernity Berners is being a little economical with the truth. The music is frequently modern harmonically, although this is a reflection of Berners' musical style rather than a conscious undertaking to shock the listener with blatant atonality. The passage shown below in Ex. 6.4 shows the end of the second scene, 'Cloudland'. Here a staccato, octatonic ascent in the wind leads to a sudden and unexpected chord of E minor with a major seventh (D#) in bar 163. The seventh does not resolve onto the anticipated E natural, but continues over unison B naturals (acting as a dominant in E minor) in the lower strings, to end the passage. To Berners the term 'modern' must have suggested the recently introduced serial techniques of Schoenberg, a composer whose music he later described as an 'infertile…enclosed, dry, rocky academic valley with no issue'.[17]

Ex. 6.4: *The Triumph of Neptune*, **piano reduction, 'Cloudland', bars 160–65**

The Triumph of Neptune was very well received, with favourable reviews appearing in much of the London press. Critics enjoyed every aspect of the ballet: the pantomime theme, the quality of the dancing, and Berners' music, which to one commentator 'recall[ed] wittily all that one ever heard

---

[16] Ibid.
[17] Amory, 1998, 83.

in little provincial theatres in one's childhood'.[18] The 'Englishness' was appreciated by all. With the same writer noting 'It is heartening to realise that the Diaghilev productions now contain an item so English as *The Triumph of Neptune*',[19] it is clear that the producers had achieved their aim.

Luna Park (1930)

Commissioned by Charles Blake Cochran[20] to write a short ballet for one of his popular London Pavilion revues, Berners found inspiration for *Luna Park*, a 'fantastic ballet in one act', in a scenario devised by Boris Kochno.[21] Originally to be titled *Luna Park, or the Freaks*, the scenario concerns a freak show in which the various 'freaks' actually turn out to be perfectly normal people.[22] On receiving the commission, Berners approached Georges Balanchine – the choreographer for *The Triumph of Neptune* – at what again turned out to be a fortuitous time. Balanchine had been looking for a means of creating work for performers of the Ballets Russes who had found themselves unemployed after the death of Diaghilev on 19 August 1929, and, glad to have found a project which would achieve this, he developed his choreography for the ballet in March 1930. Décor and costumes for this first production were by the talented young English painter Christopher Wood[23] whom Berners had first met five years earlier.

The subject matter of the ballet was ideally suited to Berners. He was able to demonstrate his liking for the fantastic in a scenario based on a practical joke which goes wrong: the showman who has devised the fake freak show is shown to be a hoaxer. Berners was known to be a very keen

---

[18] Review from *The Queen*, 15 December 1926. Reprinted in McDonald, N, 1975, 343.

[19] In Ibid.

[20] C B Cochran (1872–1951) was a prominent British impresario and theatre producer who was best known for his popular musical revues. The 1930 revue ran for three weeks in Manchester before moving to London. *Luna Park* was only performed in London, so received its premiere on the revue's opening night at the London Pavilion on Thursday 27 March 1930, conducted by Charles Prentice. (See Appendix 2 for a list of performers). It was performed alongside several other short ballets and diverse entertainments.

[21] Boris Kochno (1904–1990) was a Russian writer and ballet librettist who wrote several librettos for Diaghilev's Ballets Russes. After Diaghilev's death, he continued to work in ballet, collaborating on other projects and writing books about the subject.

[22] 'Luna Park' actually existed: it was an amusement park on Coney Island, New York, created by Frederick Thompson and Elmer "Skip" Dundy in the early 1900s, and was named after Dundy's sister, Luna.

[23] 1901–30.

practical joker, but was also fond of showing people up when he knew them to be false.

The plot of the ballet, which has obvious links with, and may well be a parody of, Stravinsky's *Petrushka* (1910–11), is as follows: at a pavilion in Luna Park a showman demonstrates his freak show which comprises a man with three heads, a three-legged juggler, a one-legged ballerina and a man with six arms. Each character is displayed in his or her own special niche. The curtain falls and the showman bows, turns down the lights and retires. After he leaves, the four freaks appear from behind the curtain and turn out to be perfectly normal human beings; they decide to go out into the world and silently slip away. The showman returns and prepares for the second performance; he opens the curtains to the niches in the same order as before, but this time without looking. The fake 'freaks' have gone and left only their spare limbs, two heads and juggling balls. Laughter from the audience alerts the showman to his error, and on realising what has happened he leaps into the empty niche behind him and pulls down the curtain.

Berners' music was written with an eye to the audience likely to attend, and as such was more accessible than anything he had yet written. The 'freakish' characteristics of the protagonists are used as the starting point for musical representation, and each has a different 'theme' which is first heard when they are introduced to the audience. The showman himself also has a special theme which consists of quick dotted rhythms over a staccato, descending chromatic bass line. He is followed by the three-headed man who has a repeated figure in triple time, in which a quaver rest in the middle of bars 23–24 suggests the jerky movement of each of the three heads in turn (Ex. 6.5). Rapid ascending and descending arpeggios over an accented three-note bass suggest the three-legged juggler (Ex. 6.6), whilst the precarious equilibrium of the one-legged ballerina is shown through sudden two-note leaps, interspersed with semiquaver rests (Ex. 6.7). There is a strong resemblance between this music and the start of 'La toupie' (The Top) from Bizet's *Jeux d'enfants* (1871) (cf. Ex. 6.7 and 6.8). Berners indicates with this little in-joke that the movements of a one-legged ballerina must be limited to hopping and spinning like a top! Where such influences are identifiable in Berners' music they are invariably French in origin.

Ex. 6.5: *Luna Park*, **piano reduction, bars 22–25**[24]

Ex. 6.6: *Luna Park*, **piano reduction, bars 70–73**

Ex. 6.7: *Luna Park*, **piano reduction, bars 118–19**[25]

Ex. 6.8: Bizet, 'La toupie' from *Jeux d'enfants*, **Primo part, bars 5–8**[26]

For the final 'freak', the difficulty of controlling six arms is suggested by the hemiola alterations to a quick but simple repeated rhythm (Ex. 6.9).

---

[24] Note the prevalence of the interval of a third in the upper line.

[25] Once again this demonstrates the importance of the look of the music on the page to Berners: vertical lines here suggests the long, narrow shape of a one-legged ballerina.

[26] Reproduced by kind permission of Editions Durand.

When the four freaks dance together, features from the music of each are blended together in a clever *Allegro* (Ex. 6.10).

Ex. 6.9: *Luna Park*, **piano reduction, bars 169–72**

Ex. 6.10: *Luna Park*, **piano reduction, bars 266–69**

After they are revealed to be normal human beings, the music of the freaks is completely altered as together they dance an *Adagio*. Here Berners uses a broad string melody full of unexpected twists; the emphasis is on long legato lines, and there is a sharp contrast with the freaks' previous music. There are no sudden leaps in the melody, which mainly moves up and down in major and minor seconds (Ex. 6.11).

Ex. 6.11: *Luna Park*, **piano reduction, 'Adagio', bars 3–6**

The *Adagio* is followed by two variations – written to show off the talents of Serge Lifar and Alice Nikitina – before the 'freaks' leave Luna Park for good. The showman's opening theme returns as he re-opens each niche in turn to find that only the spare limbs and extra heads remain. Utterly humiliated, he leaps off stage in a flurry of staccato semiquavers, pulling down the curtain as he flees. Despite the limitations of a very tiny stage, the 1930 performances went ahead without a hitch and were warmly received. *The Telegraph*'s reviewer did not care for the subject matter, but thought Berners' music 'apt, clever and sometimes even original'.[27] A commentator in *The Daily Mail*, though, was much more enthusiastic, calling the production a 'delightfully original ballet in the Petroushka style, with really humorous music by Lord Berners, superbly danced by M. Serge Lifar and Mlle. Alice Nikitina'.[28]

After hearing some of the music from *Luna Park* when it was played as an interlude during the 1932 Camargo Society performances at the Savoy Theatre, Frederick Ashton devised a completely new ballet, *Foyer de danse*, inspired by the genre paintings of Degas, which used Berners' score but abandoned Kochno's libretto. The production was premiered in October 1932, at the Mercury Theatre, London, to resounding critical acclaim. Ashton was to choreograph all Berners' ballets from then on: *A Wedding Bouquet*, *Cupid and Psyche* and *Les Sirènes*.

A Wedding Bouquet (1936)

Six years after *Luna Park* was premiered Berners was to complete work on a third ballet score, based on Gertrude Stein's 1931 play *They must. Be wedded. To their wife*. His original idea had been to produce a choral piece – perhaps an opera or cantata – using Stein's words as a libretto,[29] but he rejected this in favour of ballet, perhaps because of his earlier success with the genre. *A Wedding Bouquet*, however, was to be rather different from either of his two previous ballets in that it included an on-stage chorus whose role was to comment on the unfolding action. Whether or not it was Berners' intention from the start to create a choral ballet rather than just 'borrow' the scenario from Stein's play is unclear. However, as he had written most of the music before asking Frederick Ashton[30] and Constant Lambert to assist him in the completion of a libretto, this would seem

---

[27] 'Cochran's 1930 Revue', *Daily Telegraph*, Friday 28 March, 1930, 8.

[28] Parsons, Alan: 'Mr Cochran's Best Revue', *Daily Mail*, Friday 28 March, 1930.

[29] Goodwin, 1983, 25.

[30] Ashton had worked on the Virgil Thomson/Gertrude Stein opera-ballet, *Four Saints in Three Acts*, in 1933 and so was a natural choice as the choreographer for Berners' new production.

unlikely. With both men agreeing to help, the three worked together at Faringdon to prepare the ballet for production.

In the performances a small chorus (originally ten singers) in period costume would sing lines from Stein's play whilst standing on stage alongside the action. Berners chose not to set the whole of Stein's text, but rather to select certain passages from the beginning and middle of the play as the basis of his ballet. The title was also changed, with Stein's approval, to *A Wedding Bouquet* on the grounds that the original was 'too long for advertising'.[31] In addition to helping create the scenario, Lambert took on the role of arranging Stein's words to fit Berners' music,[32] and also conducted the first performances. The settings and costumes were designed by Berners himself and were made under the supervision of William Chappell. The first performance took place on 27 April 1937 at the Sadler's Wells Theatre in London.

The scenario, which concerns a wedding set in a provincial French town towards the turn of the century, is described below:

In the garden of a farmhouse near the French town of Bellay, preparations are being made for a wedding feast. Webster, the maid, worries that things will not be ready in time. As guests begin to appear, the chorus tells us about them; Josephine, who 'may be wearing a gown newly washed and pressed', is accompanied by her friends Paul and John. Meanwhile Violet hotly pursues Ernest who rejects her advances.

Enter Julia, whom we are told 'is known as forlorn'. Utterly dejected after being abandoned by the fickle bridegroom, Julia is accompanied by her Mexican terrier, Pépé, who protects her from the advances of a male guest. Josephine tries to comfort her without success.

The bridal party approaches, and two bridesmaids dance a waltz under the bridal veil. Seeing Julia throws the harassed bridegroom into a panic, he tries to ignore her and poses with the bridal party for a photograph. Julia follows him around, though, and the amused guests begin to gossip, guessing at the situation. Pépé tries to distract the increasingly suspicious bride but Julia throws herself at the groom's feet, causing his bride to despair. Josephine, who has had far too much to drink, makes a scene and is asked to leave. The groom dances a tango with a large chorus of his former mistresses and is overjoyed that his chosen bride is less demanding than any of his previous lovers. As night falls everyone except Julia leaves, and the curtain falls as she gazes at the empty stage.

---

[31] Goodwin, 1983, 25.
[32] Kavanagh, 1996, 212.

Stein gave Berners free rein to use passages from her play as he pleased, commenting: 'Anything you want to do will be what I want you to do'.[33] The result is a text comprising a series of remarks on the unfolding action, many of which appear fragmentary and spontaneous. The aim was not to provide a coherent running commentary which would explain the movement on stage, but rather to give insights into the lives and emotional states of the protagonists in a way that would be impossible through dancing alone. The abstract nature of the comments also enabled Berners to reflect further the chaos of the situation.

Stein's writing was renowned for its repetitious and often surreal character, and in his treatment of her words in *A Wedding Bouquet* Berners remained faithful to her literary style. The score is constructed along similar lines to the play on which it is based: Berners sets small sections of text to short melodic fragments (often only two bars long) which are reiterated as the words are repeated by the chorus (see Exx. 6.12–13).

As these examples also demonstrate, the rhythm of the music is largely dictated by the natural speech patterns of the words, suggesting that Berners had at least a working libretto to hand when he was completing the score. However, there is also evidence to show that in some cases Berners/Lambert changed words to fit the rhythm of the music better, so that, for example, the line 'so the month of August' was originally 'so the month of July' in Stein's play. The technique of repeating phrases suited Berners' musical style, which was always more at ease with repetition and variation than development. The tiny, insistent, repeated phrases foreshadow the minimalist composers of the 1970s, though their true origin lies in Stein's revolutionary prose style (see Ex. 6.13).

Despite this prevalence of repeated phrases, larger-scale repeats are rare and appear only in the orchestral interludes between the scenes of the ballet. In contrast to his earlier production, *Luna Park*, each character does not have his or her own musical representation. *A Wedding Bouquet* is a longer production with a more complex scenario and larger cast; much of the action involves many characters being on stage simultaneously and if each were to have his own motive the music would become overly complex, which was never Berners' aim.

---

[33] Amory, 1998, 167.

Ex. 6.12: *A Wedding Bouquet*, vocal score, Fig. 5, bars 5–9

Ex. 6.13: *A Wedding Bouquet*, piano score, Fig. 31, bars 1–8

Generally, the vocal parts remain clearly audible; however, there are several passages in which voices enter either in fugato or with overlapping iterations of different sentences, making it more difficult to distinguish what is actually being said. Fugal entries such as the one shown below in Ex. 6.14 reflect how a single comment by one guest can quickly end up 'on everyone's lips'. Increasing overlapping entries create the impression of several people talking at once, and let the audience feel part of the crowd.

Ex. 6.14: *A Wedding Bouquet*, **piano score, Fig. 119, bars 6–10**

Previous chapters have shown how comedy was an important element in Berners' music, and in addition to the natural humour of the chaotic situation being depicted in *A Wedding Bouquet*, there are a few typically droll Berners touches in the score. Perhaps the best example comes from the beginning of the lengthy waltz section which leads to the final tango scene. In a passage strongly reminiscent of his earlier *Valses bourgeoises* (1917), and the 'Valse sentimentale' from *Trois morceaux* (1919), a deliciously ironic twist at the words 'It is going on nicely' sees the underlying harmonies seeming to indicate that nothing could be further from the truth (Ex. 6.15).

Ex. 6.15: *A Wedding Bouquet*, **piano score, Figure 82, bar 1 – Figure 83, bar 7**

Berners also appreciated the very few opportunities given in the text to provide the occasional literal representation of an evocative word. Ex. 6.16 shows how he uses flighty trills (in the flute part) at the line 'Julia may she have heard birds' to suggest that Julia's ears had not deceived her.

Ex. 6.16: *A Wedding Bouquet*, **piano score, Figure 18, bars 7–8**

The idea of explaining the abstract text was also taken on board by Frederick Ashton, for it was with his choreography that the producers aimed to tell the story of the ballet, as well as helping to bring meaning to some of the more obscure reflections of the libretto. The choreography, libretto and music complemented each other, combining to make the ballet more accessible to the audience. Although the text was unquestionably modern, the scenario, Berners' music and Ashton's choreography were typical of their time, without anything noticeably shocking, and it is most probably this combination of the familiar and the unconventional that accounted for the ballet's popularity. In-jokes amused the cast but did not prevent audiences from enjoying the production, and the action never descended so far into farce that it was unable to recover, as was to occur later with the Berners/Ashton collaboration, *Les Sirènes* (1946).

A Wedding Bouquet was an immediate success and has been the most performed (both in England and the United States) of Berners' ballets. The original London cast list is given at the end of this chapter as Ex. 6.17. Budget limitations for performances during the war dictated that it was impractical to use a chorus, and it was suggested that it might be equally as successful to have a narrator speak the libretto. For this to work the producers needed to find someone who would be able to do justice to the humorous aspects of the text and who understood the scenario completely. The ideal narrator was found in Constant Lambert, who delivered the lines from the stage, as the chorus had done before. Evidence suggests that this was even more successful than using a chorus. A narrator was used for subsequent performances in the United States, and for post-war productions in London (when it would have been perfectly possible to re-employ a chorus). One commentator has suggested that using a narrator made the words 'finally audible'.[34] Others have observed that Lambert considered it perfectly legitimate to add his own interjections: 'On one occasion the dancer playing the maid was taken aback to hear the words, "Webster, your shoes are creaking", issuing from Lambert's stage box.'[35] Lane comments that 'later reciters lacked Lambert's formidable gifts in this kind of enterprise'.[36] Considering the success of Lambert's narration of Edith Sitwell's words in Walton's *Façade* (1921) – which, notably, was staged as a ballet as well as a spoken entertainment – it is unsurprising that his role in *A Wedding Bouquet* was so well received. The 1994 recording,[37] however,

---

[34] Vaughan, 1977, 152.

[35] Goodwin, 1983, 26 (the box was actually on the stage, not at the side).

[36] In CD liner notes to *Lord Berners: Wedding Bouquet, Luna Park, March*, Marco Polo 8.223716, recorded 1994, issued 1996, 6.

[37] *Lord Berners: Wedding Bouquet, Luna Park, March*, Marco Polo 8.223716. Recorded 1994, issued 1996.

returns to the original format in using a chorus; modern recording techniques allow the words to be clearly heard, perhaps for the first time.

Berners had played a large part in producing what proved to be a very successful ballet. The achievement was to be the high point of his musical career.

Cupid and Psyche (1938–9)

Berners' penultimate collaboration with Frederick Ashton, the three-scene ballet *Cupid and Psyche* (1938–39) was premiered on 27 April 1939 at Sadler's Wells in London. Constant Lambert conducted, and the cast included Frank Staff (Cupid), 17-year-old Julia Farron (Psyche), June Brae (Venus), Michael Somes (Pan) and Margot Fonteyn (Ceres).[38] Sir Francis Rose designed the sets and costumes at Berners' request, and on 15 April 1939 *The Times* reported that a preliminary viewing of some of the fifty-six costumes, designed by Rose and made by Ira Belline, was attended by Berners, Rose, Lady Diana Cooper and Lady Cunard, amongst others.

The idea for the ballet was Berners', and he took for his plot the ancient Roman mythological tale of Cupid and Psyche as told by the Latin author Apuleius[39] in his *Metamorphoses* or *The Golden Ass*. In order to make the complicated tale more comprehensible to the audience Berners used two narrators to explain the action, though as far as one critic was concerned this did little to help. The scenario was as follows:

A Grecian King has three daughters; the youngest, Psyche, is so beautiful that people worship her rather than Venus. Enraged, Venus sends her son, Cupid, to find Psyche and reap revenge by making her fall in love with the ugliest possible man. Beneath the mask of invisibility, however, Cupid falls in love with Psyche and takes her away to a palace where the Zephyrs attend her. Cupid remains invisible; conditions imposed on the union of Gods and mortals mean that he must only visit under cover of night. To look at him, Psyche is warned, would lead to disaster.

Psyche misses her sisters, so Cupid allows the Zephyrs to bring them to the palace. They soon become envious and claim that Cupid must be a hideous monster, driven only by lust. Disturbed by her sisters' claims, Psyche takes a lamp to Cupid's bedside and sees he is a sweet, gentle

---

[38] See Appendix 2 for a full cast list.
[39] Apuleius, born c.124 AD, died after 170 AD.

creature. A drop of oil falls on his shoulder waking him, and, reproaching Psyche for her lack of faith, he flies away.

While Venus holds Cupid captive, Psyche wanders through many countries in search of him. After undergoing many trials and persecutions sent by Venus, she eventually gives up and returns home. Determined to end her suffering she goes to cast herself into the sea, but just then the God Pan appears and calls upon the other Gods to help. Ceres, Minerva, Apollo, Diana, Jupiter and Juno plead with Venus to relent which, eventually, she does, allowing Cupid and Psyche to marry at last.

By accounts, this was a rather unconventional production, and this, in part, may explain its very marked lack of success: Cupid and Psyche danced in blue and lime-yellow costumes, Jupiter in magentas and pinks and Minerva in a plastic black horsehair costume. Venus was coquettish and far from divine; Juno a pantomime dame and Jupiter a caricature of a goose-stepping dictatorial leader, complete with fascist salute. In the comical moments, Ashton's choreography included cartwheels, while at other times it was much more straight-laced. One reviewer thought the serious choreography to be rather self-conscious, 'as though it would have been decently and humourlessly classical if only the music would have allowed; and the dancers, as a consequence, seemed restive, too, and a little strained'.[40] The humour that the producers were aiming for descended, especially in the final scene, into a desperate farce which did not suit the seriousness of the plot and did not go down well with critics or audiences. A writer for *The Manchester Guardian* spoke of 'Lord Berners' nimbly disrespectful mind'[41] and added, 'never can ballet have made less attempt to take this cherished story seriously than was done to-night at Sadler's Wells'.[42]

In April 1939, when a full-scale European war was looming ever larger on the horizon, frivolity seemed inappropriate. Berners, Ashton and Rose had seriously misjudged popular feeling and the ballet was a total flop. Despite the judgement in *The Times* that on the whole, 'the "Ayes" had it',[43] and a laudatory review in *The Daily Telegraph* which claimed that 'Cupid and Psyche is a charming ballet, and the audience appreciated it to

---

[40] *The Manchester Guardian*, Friday 28 April 1939.
[41] Ibid.
[42] Ibid.
[43] 'Mixed reception', *The Times*, 28 April 1939.

the full',[44] *Cupid and Psyche* lasted for only five performances,[45] and remains unpublished.

The music of *Cupid and Psyche* deserves reassessment; failings in the original production stemmed from a combination of factors and should not deter us from investigating Berners' contribution. The comment of one reviewer that 'Lord Berners's score...never quite surrenders its querulous acid tone even when the lovers are dancing their enraptured pas de deux'[46] is unfair. The music is varied and entertaining; a lively overture sounds as though it has escaped from *The Triumph of Neptune*, and its British band-music feel, complete with side drums and strident brass themes, must have made the audiences wonder if they were in the right theatre. There are the usual waltzes (Berners slid into waltz form with great regularity and ease), and a magical entr'acte between scenes 1 and 2, whose mood and woodwind ostinati are strikingly similar to the 'Prelude' from *Fantaisie Espagnole*. A flute and glockenspiel melody runs through this entr'acte and has a simplicity and tenderness not overly common in Berners' music, but most welcome nevertheless. Perhaps the reason why some critics were unenthusiastic was that the music did not 'fit' their ideas of what would suit a ballet based on a classical tale. If a new libretto could be devised, as it was for a new production of Berners' puppet ballet *L'Uomo dai baffi* in 1998,[47] the music of *Cupid and Psyche* could have a new lease of life.

Les Sirènes (1946)

Completed in July 1946, Berners' final ballet, *Les Sirènes* was originally to be titled *Seagulls*; it then became *Sirens and Seagulls*[48] before finally being changed to *Les Sirènes*. Set on the French Riviera at the turn of the century – 'when spirits were high and skirts were long'[49] – it received its first

---

[44] Richard Capell, 'Lord Berners's New Ballet', *The Daily Telegraph*, 28 April 1939, 12.

[45] Lane claims that the ballet ran for four performances (CD liner notes to *Lord Berners Ballet Music: Les Sirènes, Cupid and Psyche, Caprice péruvien*, Marco Polo, 8.223780, recorded 1994-1995, issued 1995, 9), Amory that it ran for three performances (1998, 177). However, *The Times* for April–May 1939 clearly lists performances on the following days: Thursday 27 April, Friday 28 April, Saturday 29 April, Monday 1 May, Tuesday 2 May.

[46] JHM, *The Manchester Guardian*, Friday 28 April 1939.

[47] See Chapter 7.

[48] Lane suggests this possible early title was in French, *La plage; ou les Sirènes*, (CD liner notes to *Lord Berners Ballet Music: Les Sirènes, Cupid and Psyche, Caprice péruvien*, Marco Polo, 8.223780, recorded 1994–1995, issued 1995, 5).

[49] 'Les Sirènes', *The Times*, 13 November 1946.

performance on 12 November 1946, at the Royal Opera House; the first new ballet produced by Sadler's Wells after its move to Covent Garden. The cast included Margot Fonteyn as La Bolero, Leslie Edwards as her Chauffeur-accompanist, Frederick Ashton as King Hihat of Agpar[50] and Robert Helpmann as 'Adelino Canberra (of the Adelaide opera)'.[51] The initial idea for the ballet had come from Ashton, and besides taking a leading role in the production he was also the choreographer. His aim had been to create a ballet that combined elements of a novel, *Moths* (1880), by the English novelist Ouida,[52] with figures from the world of celebrity, and with seagulls, whose flight patterns fascinated him. Cecil Beaton designed the Edwardian costumes and scenery.

Containing some of Berners' most accessible music, the score mixes folk dances – a mazurka, farruca and habanera – with a pas de deux and numerous waltzes (his favourite dance form). Within each set piece, he uses his standard technique of repeating thematic material rather than developing it, creating contrast by changing the orchestration. The influence of Debussy and Ravel is clear – especially in the opening Prelude (where echoes of *La mer* and *Prélude à l'après midi d'un faune* are easily detected) and in the opening scene which follows. Berners stamped his own modern and mischievous mark on everything, however, with 'wrong-note' melodies similar to ones heard in the *Valses bourgeoises*, in a waltz near the end of *A Wedding Bouquet*, and in 'Valse sentimentale' from *Trois morceaux*, frequently turning up in the waltzes here.

The curtain rises on the opening scene to show a beach where sirens[53] are sitting on a rock and two seagulls search among the sands. It is dawn, and oscillating background arpeggios have the same atmospheric effect as the opening of 'Lever du jour' from Ravel's second *Daphnis et Chloé* suite. The sirens are combing their hair and singing a waltz (actually sung by a chorus of women's voices). As a group of children appear, the sirens and seagulls are scared away and in a lively staccato passage the children play while their nurses flirt with the local gendarmes. The seagulls return, and

---

[50] According to Kavanagh, King Hihat was modelled on King Farouk of Egypt. Lady Kitty was based on Lady Dolly and Adelino Canberra on Raphael Corrèze: two characters from Ouida's 1880 novel, *Moths*, which had provided much of the inspiration behind the ballet.

[51] The similarity of this name with the pseudonym, Adela Quèbec, under which Berners had privately published his 1935 novel *The Girls of Radcliff Hall*, (a pseudonym which in turn alluded to Angela Brazil) points to just one of the 'in jokes' which littered *Les Sirènes*.

[52] Pseudonym of Maria Louise (de la) Ramé(e) (1839–1908).

[53] The sirens were mermaids (as in European folklore), rather than the half-bird, half-woman sirens from Greek mythology.

finding that the sirens have left behind their combs, they begin to preen each other's feathers.

The 'fashionable folk' – celebrities and eccentrics – arrive on the scene and parade around in a bold waltz. Countess Kitty dances a mazurka and flirts with both Captain Bay Vavasour and an 'in vogue' tenor, Adelino Canberra, after which echoes of the previous waltz return. A horn call signals the appearance of 'an intense Spanish ballerina',[54] La Bolero, a caricature of La Belle Otéro,[55] and, after a brief quote from the opening bars of the first of Waldteufel's popular *Estudiantina* waltzes,[56] she tops Kitty's mazurka by dancing a lively farruca. This energetic dance, reminiscent of Berners' earlier *Fantaisie Espagnole*, entrances the captain and tenor, although only the tenor has caught La Bolero's eye.

A foreign aristocrat, King Hihat of Agpar (Frederick Ashton wearing a fez) appears[57] and flirts with La Bolero in an 'Allegro agitato' as a cor anglais and oboe weave 'eastern' sounding themes over a mysterious string accompaniment. Countess Kitty jealously takes her leave and the three rivals for La Bolero's love attempt to charm her; the guardsman, in a strident brass passage, offers marriage, the disloyal tenor his love and the King his jewels. La Bolero opts for the jewels, although her heart belongs to the 'sentimental but not very courageous'[58] tenor. They leave the stage, but as soon as the others are out of sight La Bolero returns to do a slow habanera with the tenor. A contralto sings a love song before the previously heard quote from the first of Waldteufel's *Estudiantina* waltzes reappears.

In a pas de deux, La Bolero, carried away, drops King Hihat's jewels; not realising what she has done, she goes for a swim with the tenor to cool off. As the pair head for the sea the two seagulls find the jewels on the sand, carry them off to a rock and fall asleep. Mechanical waves are brought onto the stage by the corps de ballet and everyone bathes until

---

[54] 'Les Sirènes', *The Dancing Times*, December 1946, 114.

[55] Caroline Otéro (1868–1965) was a famous Spanish dancer and courtesan in Europe and America at the turn of the century. Among her lovers were European royalty and wealthy businessmen.

[56] Emile Waldteufel (1837–1915) was a French composer, pianist and conductor. He was appointed court pianist to Napoleon III from 1865 and became the conductor of state balls the following year. He was renowned as a composer for writing over 180 waltzes, which included *Les patineurs* (1882), *Estudiantina* (1883) and *Espana* (1886). Many enjoyed a lasting popularity.

[57] Kavanagh recounts how Ashton's entry onto the stage on the first night was made in a hot air balloon; he suffered vertigo and promptly forgot his steps in the following dance (1996, 327).

[58] 'Les Sirènes', *The Dancing Times*, December 1946, 114.

sirens rise out of the water causing enough confusion to empty the beach of all but La Bolero and the tenor. King Hihat returns from his afternoon nap, discovers La Bolero and the tenor embracing, and demands back his jewels. When they cannot be found Lady Kitty calls the police, whereupon the tenor hides! In the ensuing scandal, everyone, including the tenor,[59] scorns La Bolero as she is arrested and leaves the stage in a big yellow car. Themes from previous movements are brought together in this dénouement, with echoes of the beginning of the pas de deux along with a passage first heard when the tenor tried to charm La Bolero, and several further references to Waldteufel's first *Estudiantina* waltz.

As the evening draws on, the sirens reappear on the rock. The gulls, who have seen the day's events unravel, play with the jewels and the male adorns the female with diamonds. In a return of the music from the opening scene, she preens herself as the sirens sing in the background. A distant waltz softly hints at earlier theme, but the day is over. The curtain falls to a last descending scale in the orchestra, before a sudden crescendo leads to the final *forte* chord.

Critical reaction to *Les Sirènes* was mixed. Berners' score, described as 'aqueous and romantic'[60] was acclaimed by a reviewer for *The Times* who commented: 'Lord Berners's music is a pastiche of every style required by the period and plot of his scenario, which it therefore fits like a glove.'[61] His review also commended the work of Ashton, Beaton and the dancers, ending with glowing praise: 'A hundred details adorned this fantasia, and increased its gaiety. A hundred more remain to be discovered among its riches.'[62] Critics were unanimous in their praise for Margot Fonteyn, who, according to one, '"out-Spain[ed]" the most Spanish of dancers'.[63] Enthusiasm for Robert Helpmann's singing voice (as the operatic tenor he was required to sing, albeit only briefly) was rather less emphatic. Despite *The Times* laudatory review, other commentators seemed to find the production rather laboured. The jokes lasted a little too long, and everyone seemed to be trying so hard to be funny that any sense of wittiness was somehow lost in the process. In-jokes, which amused the cast, did not go down well with ballet audiences, and it seems for many the production was too 'over-the-top'. Steyn describes the problems:

---

[59] Ashton made several drafts of the synopsis, and in another version he had the La Bolero *and* the tenor leave the stage weeping. (See Kavanagh, 1996, 326.)
[60] 'Les Sirènes', *The Times,* 13 November 1946, 8.
[61] Ibid.
[62] Ibid.
[63] 'Les Sirènes', *The Dancing Times*, December 1946, 114.

Serious ballet-goers were slightly taken aback at the gimmick laden, everything-but-the-kitchen-sink production: a big yellow motor car was brought on, Frederick Ashton came down in a balloon, Robert Helpmann sang…the merits of the ballet were lost among the trickery.[64]

To add insult to injury, the English composer and arranger Roy Douglas (b.1907) claimed to have been employed, in September 1945, to orchestrate *Les Sirènes* and spoke out bitterly against Berners. A composer mainly for film and television, Douglas was better known as an arranger. He formed associations with Vaughan Williams (from 1944 until Vaughan Williams' death in 1958) and Walton (between 1940 and 1976) helping both to prepare works for performance and publication. He orchestrated Addinsell's film scores between 1937 and 1945, including that of *Dangerous Moonlight* (1941) which contained the famous *Warsaw Concerto*.

Although apparently sworn to secrecy about his work on Berners' final ballet score, a poor salary of £160 and no mention in the programme on the opening night caused Douglas to complain. His claim to have received very little input from Berners, despite visiting him on four occasions to discuss the orchestration, is difficult to substantiate, but his allegation that the short sections already orchestrated by Berners before his own involvement were 'amateurish and ineffective'[65] reeks of sour grapes. Berners' skills in orchestration had been proved long before *Les Sirènes* had even been conceived. The truth behind the affair will remain a mystery, but the animosity, combined with tepid audience receptions, made this a sad ending to Berners' career in writing for the musical stage.

The score remains unpublished[66] and the ballet ran for only nineteen performances, after which it was not revived. As one of the most entertaining and absorbing of his ballet scores, it is both surprising and regrettable that *Les Sirènes* did not achieve the acclaim it deserved during Berners' lifetime.

****

Although Berners' ballets vary considerably in terms of their length, subject matter and size of cast and orchestra, there are many similarities in

---

[64] Steyn, 1983, 32–33.

[65] Amory, 1998, 226.

[66] Despite being unpublished both *Les Sirènes* and *Cupid and Psyche* were recorded and issued on CD in 1995.

style which help identify them as being *his* works. Unlike his earlier piano music and songs, all were written in the knowledge that they would be subject to great public interest and scrutiny. Although not musically insubstantial by any means, the tone of each ballet remains light, with an emphasis on comedy which is most prevalent in *A Wedding Bouquet*. Previous chapters examining his piano music and songs also revealed a strong inclination towards humour, and Berners' ballets are written in the same vein but on a much larger and more public scale. What we know about Berners' character makes his choice of ballet subjects – practical jokes, fantastical or farcical situations – unsurprising.

In keeping with Berners' earlier works, in which he drew on the characteristics of Spanish (*Fantaisie espagnole*), Russian ('Kasatchok' from *Trois morceaux*) and Chinese ('Chinoiserie' from *Trois morceaux*) music, as well as imitating the idiosyncrasies of the individual composers discussed in previous chapters, there are passages of pastiche in each ballet. These are always an affectionate imitation of other composers' styles, and demonstrate that Berners was highly skilled and sympathetic in his approach. The music of each ballet is accessible though not harmonically simple and different musical styles frequently appear in close proximity. One scene in *The Triumph of Neptune*, for example, begins with an imitation of English pastoral music and ends with an octatonic ascent to an unresolved dissonant chord. Because of the nature of ballet, with its changing scenes and characters, the successive use of different musical styles in this way never strikes the listener as being inappropriate.

Michael Hurd accurately describes Berners' musical style as mixing 'irony, satire and a degree of submerged romanticism'.[67] The sense of romanticism, though, is often more evident than the word 'submerged' suggests and passages such as the 'Adagio' from *Luna Park* and 'Cloudland' from *The Triumph of Neptune* are some of the most natural and unaffected that Berners ever wrote. It is this mixture of moments of romantic indulgence with frequently atonal but light-hearted jollity that best sums up Berners' musical character; simply to take one style or the other would be to hear only half the story.

---

[67] In CD liner notes to *Lord Berners: Songs, Piano Music*, Marco Polo 8.225159, recorded 1998, issued 2000, 2.

A WEDDING BOUQUET

Webster   ("Webster was a name that was spoken")   Ninette de Valois
                                                              afterwards Sheila McCarthy

Two Peasant Girls   Linda Sheridan, Joan Leaman
Two Peasant Boys   ("They must hurry and get their waggon")   Paul Reymond,
                                                                        Alan Carter

Josephine   (" She may be wearing a gown newly washed and pressed")   June Brae
Paul   (" Pleasant, vivacious and quarrelsome")   Harold Turner
John   (" An elder brother who regrets the illness of his father") William Chappell
Violet   ("She may be delightful or not, as it happens")   Pamela May
Ernest   ("May be a victim of himself")   Claude Newman
Thérèse   ("Will be faintly neat")   Elizabeth Miller
Julia   ("Is known as forlorn")   Margot Fonteyn

Bridegroom   ("They all speak as if they expected him not to be charming")
                                                               Robert Helpmann
Pépé (Julia's Dog)   ("Little dogs resemble girls")   Julia Farron
Arthur   ("Very well, I thank you")   Leslie Edwards
Guy   ("unknown")   Michael Somes
Four Guests   ("They incline to oblige only when they stare") Gwyneth Mathews,
                               Wenda Horsburgh, Joy Newton, Anne Spicer
Two Gendarmes   ("They may recognise places")   Paul Reymond,
                                                                        Alan Carter
Bride   ("Charming! Charming! Charming!")   Mary Honer
Bridesmaids   ("They make preparations to deal with an exception") Molly Brown,
                                                                        Jill Gregory

Members of the Opera Company:
Misses Teychenne, Jackson, Strudwick, Carline, Lewtas, Tollworthy.
Messrs. Tree, Mossop, Cannon, Barber

Conductor: Constant Lambert

Ex. 6.17: Cast list for first performance of *A Wedding Bouquet* [68]

---

[68] The cast list for the programmes was designed by Constant Lambert who added descriptions for the characters from Stein's play; not all of the descriptions are heard during the course of the ballet.

Chapter 7

In Retrospect

The Triumph of Neptune and *A Wedding Bouquet* were the high points of Berners' musical career, and the critical acclaim that he enjoyed with them was never repeated. The failure of his next ballet, *Cupid and Psyche*, was the first such blow Berners was to receive and it is significant that after this he turned his attentions towards other, non-musical interests. Even before *Cupid and Psyche*, Berners had been investigating other creative avenues: he held his second exhibition of paintings in May 1936 at the Lefevre Gallery, London, and wrote two short novels, *The Camel* (1936) and *The Girls of Radcliff Hall* (1937).

As mentioned in Chapter 1, the onset of World War II caused Berners to have a nervous breakdown. For a man whose outlook was essentially a cosmopolitan one – he had homes in England and Italy, and frequently stayed in France and Germany – such an international conflict had serious implications for his whole way of life. He was prone to bouts of depression from an early age, but this was the most severe breakdown he ever suffered, and the only one seriously to impede his creativity. Berners moved to Oxford where he took up a job as a cataloguer of foreign books at the Taylorian Institute; the only music he attempted to write at this time consisted of exercises in counterpoint.[1] His depression lasted several weeks, but by the end of 1939 Berners was back at Faringdon. Over the next few years, though, his creative output slowed right down. He produced only a couple of comic songs, *Red Noses and Red Roses* (c.1940) and *Come on Algernon* (1943), and a handful of pieces for solo piano: *Polka* (1941),[2] *Valse* (1943),[3] and *The Expulsion from Paradise* (1945).[4] The latter was written to accompany a nativity play produced by Penelope Betjeman. These works bear little relation to Berners' early piano music and songs: the piano pieces are far simpler harmonically and comparatively longer

---

[1] Many of these survive and are held at the British Library, along with the manuscripts for most of his other works: see Appendix 2.

[2] Written as incidental music to a pantomime called *Cinderella, or There's Many a Slipper*, performed on 29 December 1941, at Radcliffe Infirmary, Oxford. The *Polka* was played on two pianos by Tom Bell and Lionel Grunbaum.

[3] Part of this was later re-used in Berners' film score for *The Halfway House*.

[4] See Appendix 2 for further details.

than his earlier writings. The two comic songs were intended purely as frivolous entertainment, rather than serious contributions to his musical output. Although written very late in his career as a composer these works are far less forward-looking than his earlier music. An interest in writing had occupied Berners' creative activities, too, with five short novels (*Far from the Madding War, Count Omega, Percy Wallingford, Mr Pidger*, and *The Romance of a Nose*) being published in 1941.

In the end it was Ernest Irving, musical director of Ealing Studios, who persuaded Berners to return to larger-scale musical composition. In 1943 he asked him to provide the film score for *The Halfway House*, a rather creepy, supernatural tale about events that occur at an inn in which the hotel owner and his daughter turn out to be ghosts. Irving was a composer himself and, according to Amory, 'he approached practically all the interesting composers of the time, [obtaining] film scores from, among others, William Walton, Vaughan Williams, John Ireland, Alan Rawsthorne, Richard Addinsell and the Frenchman Georges Auric'.[5] Although this was a new genre for Berners, many of the skills required for a successful film score were already familiar to him: 'His experience of writing ballet music, with its need to produce brief, precisely timed supporting passages, was...helpful'.[6] The score was a success and Berners was later asked to provide two numbers for the film *Champagne Charlie* (1944) and another complete score for *Nicholas Nickleby* (1947). For *Champagne Charlie* he re-used the earlier *Polka* and bawdy song *Come on Algernon* ('Come on Algernon, that's not enough for me. Give me some more, the same as before, because I can't count under three').

Berners' film score for the 1947 Ealing production of Dickens' 1838–39 novel *Nicholas Nickleby* was to be his final musical work. The film, directed by Alberto Cavalcanti (1897–1982),[7] was premiered in November 1947. Ernest Irving commissioned Berners to write the music, orchestrated the piano score and conducted the Philharmonia Orchestra's performance of it for the film's soundtrack. As an acknowledgement of the contribution Irving had made, the incidental music, published as a piano reduction by Chappell in 1947, was dedicated to him.

Films based on classic works of literature are frequently condemned as being too short to convey adequately all aspects of the book upon which they are based. Condensing a detailed book into film format is

---

[5] Amory, 1998, 216.
[6] Ibid., 217.
[7] Cavalcanti had also directed *Champagne Charlie* (1944).

understandably a difficult process and unfortunately Cavalcanti's film suffered greatly from the action progressing too rapidly. Dickens' novel had first appeared serialised in twenty monthly parts, so when made into a film of an hour and forty minutes it is not surprising that details were lost. Several characters critical to the unravelling of the plot in the novel became peripheral in the film, making the action unfold, at times, in an illogical way. The protagonists were over-simplified, making them seem rather too one-sided to be plausible. In short, the viewer is given a whistle-stop tour through Nicholas' adventures and the result is disappointing. The film did not receive favourable critical acclaim when first released, but the criticisms were not directed at Berners' score which is at all times perfectly adequate, if not particularly striking or new. His background in ballet music gave Berners a firm foundation in producing timed set pieces, although film music written to accompany on-screen action and dialogue required an even greater precision from composer and conductor.[8] The score for *Nicholas Nickleby* responded to the drama as efficiently as would have been expected from a composer of Berners' experience, in fact it was one of the redeeming features of the film.

Berners' last few major musical works, *Cupid and Psyche, Les Sirènes* and *Nicholas Nickleby*, sadly proved less prestigious than might have been expected and were a disappointingly flat end to a career that, over a span of thirty years, had seen some considerable musical achievements. Having suffered deteriorating health for a number of years, Berners died at Faringdon on 19 April 1950 at the age of 66.

Obituaries appeared throughout the national and music press, even appearing in several foreign journals.[9] *The Musical Times* summarised his career, describing Berners as 'a skilful and witty composer, a modernist with a penchant for the bizarre, and...a most successful parodist'.[10] However, an editorial comment in *The Strad* would undoubtedly have pleased him rather more:

The recent death of Lord Berners has deprived us of one of the most striking artistic personalities of the day. His versatility was remarkable since he made

---

[8] This is reflected in the number of drafts Berners rejected before producing the final version of the score. These drafts are held at the British Library.

[9] *The Music Index* from 1950 cites six obituaries: in *Billboard*, lxii, 52, *Monthly Musical Record*, lxxx, 190, *Musical America*, lxx, 26, *Musical Courier*, cxli, 25, *Musical Times*, xci, 198 and *The Strad*, lxi, 43.

[10] 'Obituary' in *The Musical Times*, xci, 198.

his name both as a writer and a painter, though it is chiefly as a composer of music that he will be remembered.[11]

However, in the years following Berners' death his music disappeared from public view. References to him in *The Music Index*[12] show that interest in his music suffered a decline between 1951 and 1969, when only five related articles appeared in the major music journals.

The reasons for this dwindling of interest are manifold, but perhaps the most significant is that the musical forms Berners preferred were unlikely to retain much public attention. Small-scale piano music and songs rarely reach a particularly large audience, ballet music only if regularly performed as a concert work, rather than stage production. It is also significant that the best-known English composers of the twentieth century, Vaughan Williams, Elgar and Tippett, all wrote symphonies, and if evidence of the level of public interest in this particular genre is required, the excitement over Anthony Payne's completion of Elgar's third symphony[13] should be proof enough. Lord FitzCricket's comment in *Far from the Madding War* that 'The English have a tendency to judge art by size and weight'[14] proved to be highly apt. It is likely, therefore, that much of Berners' music was never particularly well known in wider public circles. Previous chapters have shown that he favoured modification and variation over thematic development throughout his musical career, so a large-scale symphony would have been completely alien to his style. In view of his lack of formal training, it was also most probably outside his capabilities. Crucially, though, his elevated social position meant that Berners did not need to compose to earn money and so the necessity of creating works with mass appeal never arose for him. Although his ballets and film music show that he was perfectly able to write more 'accessible' music, the ballets in particular are rather deceptive in this respect: their tunefulness often belies the harmonic complexity of the score which analysis soon identifies. Once he discovered his ideal medium in ballet he did not look back, but although there was plenty of press interest in the premieres of the staged productions, performances of the ballet scores as concert works did not occur regularly in music venues (with the exception of the 'Suite' from *The Triumph of Neptune*) and so soon disappeared from public view.

---

[11] 'Editorial notes' in *The Strad*, lxi, no.722 (1950), 43.

[12] A subject-author index of music periodical literature, published annually since 1949.

[13] First performed on 15 February 1998, at the Royal Festival Hall, London, by the BBC Symphony Orchestra, conducted by Andrew Davis.

[14] 1941, 164.

It is possible to draw parallels between Berners and other composers of the 1920s, the most important being Stravinsky and the members of Les Six. Indeed comparisons here indicate that Berners was perhaps fortunate to see his popularity last until the onset of World War II. He was not as versatile, wide-ranging or original as Stravinsky, had no deepening experience via religious conversion (as with Poulenc in 1936), nor was as prolific as Milhaud (to whom the odd failure was of lesser consequence). The best parallel is perhaps with Auric in whose varied career ballets and film scores also played an important role. In England, Constant Lambert, a firm friend of Berners, was the only other British composer to be commissioned by Diaghilev to write for the Ballets Russes. Although Lambert assisted Berners with the arrangement of words to music in *A Wedding Bouquet* his own musical outlook was far more 'serious', so similarities in compositional style are few.

At the beginning of the twenty-first century Berners is best remembered for his 'parodies', and these have tended to overshadow his other, more substantial, achievements. An anonymous short essay[15] on his work, published (in English with a French translation) by Chester in 1923, bemoaned the fact that few critics appreciated his importance in bringing a 'new spirit...into the art of music. By the majority he was at once pigeon-holed, and they attached the tag of 'musical humorist' to him, ready for reference on the appearance of every subsequent work'.[16] Although this essay was written very early in Berners' musical career, the commentator identified a label which would remain forever associated with his work. There is no doubt, however, that Berners was highly skilled at writing such music. The same writer comments: 'not content with a mere reproduction of the idioms of others, [Berners] holds up in front of them the distorting mirror of his own invention and thus caricatures their shape, which remains recognisable, but is imprinted with the caricaturist's own personality'.[17] Nonetheless, it is unfortunate that this tag of 'humorist' or 'parodist' seems to have stuck to the extent that certain music dictionaries make no mention of his ballet scores whatsoever. One comments: 'Berners affected bizarre social behaviour; his humour and originality are reflected in his compositions, many of which reveal a subtle gift for parody.'[18] This seems to imply that his skills as a parodist are the only aspect of Berners' work

---

[15] Possibly by Dr Arthur Eaglefield Hull (see Bibliography).
[16] 1923, 4.
[17] Ibid., 6.
[18] Slonimsky, N ed., *Baker's Bibliographical Dictionary of Musicians*, 1992, 172.

worthy of note, which is patently untrue. Previous chapters have shown how Berners' musical personality was a striking and novel one, and though he had an unquestionable talent for imitating and reconstructing the styles of others in his own unique way, there is more originality to his music than this entry would suggest. In any case, to describe Berners' imitative works as 'parodies' is not altogether appropriate. *The Concise Oxford Dictionary* defines parody as 'a humorous exaggerated imitation of an author, literary work, or style', or as 'a feeble imitation'.[19] In works where Berners imitates other composers or musical styles the intention is to create an affectionate pastiche not an exaggerated jibe, and his compositions are certainly never feeble. This makes it even more unfortunate that the label of 'parodist' is so often attached to his name.

Berners' music often reflects his sense of humour, which at different times favoured either wit or the sort of base comedy displayed in 'Du bist wie eine Blume'. Here the piano accompaniment imitates the grunts of the pig, by whom, according to Berners, Heine's poem was inspired. The impact of Berners' interpretation is heightened by the seriousness of the numerous other, well-known settings of this text. The ballets *Luna Park* and *A Wedding Bouquet* show Berners' love of farce and sense of schadenfreude when the central characters – the showman and bridegroom – each get their come-uppance. Berners' choice of Prosper Mérimée's comic play *Le carrosse du Saint-sacrement* as the text for his only opera was another early indication of the importance to him of humour in music.

Despite his childhood fascination with Wagner, Berners found his mature musical ideal to be the antithesis of the German tradition. His preference for clarity, precision, and directness of expression mirrored that of Ravel, with whom he also shared a fondness for dance forms, particularly the waltz. Occasionally referred to as the 'English Satie', Berners shared with the older French composer a penchant for quirky titles, a preference for brevity, a love of the bizarre and a tendency towards droll humour. Both were serious eccentrics, although Berners' musical language was more sophisticated than Satie's. Berners' major musical influence was undoubtedly Stravinsky but if it is necessary to identify a nationality in Berners' music then his outlook, harmonic language and musical objectives best fit with his French contemporaries in Les Six, several of whom were equally influenced by the Russian genius.

---

[19] *The Concise Oxford Dictionary of Current English* (London, BCA, 1/1911;8/1993, 866).

Berners' musical style is frequently described as 'cosmopolitan' and this is accurate not only because he demonstrated the ability to set different languages sympathetically in his songs, but also because he combined different musical systems – atonality, diatonicism, chromaticism and octatonicism – without the juxtapositions ever seeming inappropriate. In addition, his directness of expression means that there is little extraneous 'padding', and the musical thought is always focused and distinct.

There is something of a dichotomy in Berners' style, though, which sees a division between the heart-felt music of, for example, the 'Lullaby' from *Three English Songs* or the 'Adagio' from *Luna Park*, and the more impersonal expression of much of his other music. This is not to suggest that his other works are emotionally detached, but many are less overtly Romantic. Though we can detect compassion in 'Pour un canari' from *Trois petites marches funèbres*, or in *Le poisson d'or*, in each case Berners aims to lessen the impact of the emotion by diverting our sympathies onto an unlikely subject: in both pieces, an animal rather than a person. It is as if he aims to erect a barrier between himself and any outward display of affection – he often deflects sentiment through humour – so on the occasions where he displays real empathy for the human condition, his music is at its most profound.

The 'Lullaby' from *Three English Songs*, is a good example of this. The simple stillness of the accompaniment together with the relatively straightforward melodic line reflects the innocence of the child, to whom it is sung. This simplicity is even more apparent when the song is compared to the second from the same set, 'The Lady Visitor in the Pauper Ward'. Here the anguish and torment of the speaker is reflected through jagged melodic lines, chromatic slides, strident discords and unexpected accents. Although very different in effect, both songs reflect aspects of the human experience and it is no coincidence that both are particularly striking in their own way. Berners tends to use music which is harmonically straightforward when he is expressing a sense of pathos, the previously mentioned 'Adagio' from *Luna Park* being a good example. However, 'The Lady Visitor in the Pauper Ward', along with 'La haine' from the *Fragments psychologiques*, show that when the sentiment is darker or more pessimistic Berners uses a more complex harmonic language. This latter work contains the darkest music that Berners ever wrote and is also one of his most harmonically obscure creations.

****

Between 1970 and 1988, there was a noticeable revival of interest in Berners' work, which is reflected by the increased number of references in *The Music Index*.[20] On 8 December 1972 an 'Evening of Lord Berners' – a concert of his piano music and songs later broadcast twice by the BBC, on 12 December 1973 and 20 April 1975 – was recorded in the Purcell Room, and this played a substantial role in bringing Berners' music back into public view. *A Wedding Bouquet* was revived for the Lilian Baylis Centenary gala in 1974,[21] and again in October 1983, at Covent Garden, to celebrate the centenary of Berners' birth. A Centenary Exhibition of his work was also held at the Royal Festival Hall, ending on the 17 November 1983. The same year also saw the first BBC broadcasts of the ballet *Les Sirènes*[22] and the opera *Le carrosse du Saint-sacrement*,[23] and, the following year, a suite from *Cupid and Psyche*.[24] In 1979 David Bintley created a new ballet, *Punch and the Street Party* for Sadler's Wells Royal Ballet, using music from *The Triumph of Neptune* with some additional numbers by Philip Lane. Newly collected volumes of Berners' solo piano and vocal music, edited by Peter Dickinson, appeared in 1980,[25] and came back into print in 2001 after several years of being available only as authorised photocopies from the publishers.

The year 1987 saw the broadcast of a dramatised version of the novel *Count Omega*,[26] in which the accompanying music was *L'Uomo dai baffi*. Three years later, in 1990, *A Wedding Bouquet* was performed at the Proms.[27] Since 1994, almost all Berners' ballets, piano music, songs and orchestral works have been newly recorded and issued on CD. In 1998, Berners' music for his puppet ballet *L'Uomo dai baffi* was brought back to public view in a new production with the same title, though now with real

---

[20] Between 1970 and 1988 there are 15 references.

[21] It had also been heard at the Sadler's Wells twenty-first anniversary gala in 1951.

[22] 14 December 1983, BBC Scottish Symphony Orchestra, conducted by Nicholas Cleobury.

[23] 18 September 1983, soloists: Ian Caddy, Alexander Oliver, Cynthia Buchan, John Winfield, Thomas Lawlor, and Anthony Smith. BBC Scottish Symphony Orchestra, conducted by Nicholas Cleobury. The recording was only issued on CD in 2000 (see Appendix 4: Discography).

[24] 13 January 1984, Ulster Orchestra conducted by Nicholas Cleobury.

[25] These included several works appearing in print for the first time: *Dispute entre le papillon et le crapaud* (1914–15), *Polka* (1941), *Valse* (1943), *March* (c1945), *The Expulsion from Paradise* (1945), *Red Roses and Red Noses* (c1940), and *Come on Algernon* (1944).

[26] 10 March 1987. Nicholas Cleobury conducted the Aquarius Ensemble. The dramatisation was by Mike Steer.

[27] 3 March 1990.

dancers rather than puppets. The choreography was by Mark Baldwin and the production was nominated in the 'Best New Dance Production' category in the 1999 Laurence Olivier Awards. Reviews were positive; one commentator noted: 'It was quirky and likeable (like Lord Berners' music) without necessarily being very substantial.'[28] Another critic described it as 'a witty and humorous slice of the surreal, taking inspiration from Andrew Flint-Shipman's paintings and the eccentricity of the music of Lord Berners'.[29]

Mark Amory's important biography of Berners was published in 1998, and in the week of 17–21 April 2000, Berners had the posthumous honour of being BBC Radio 3's 'Composer of the Week'. Five hour-long programmes dedicated to his music were broadcast, marking (although this was not actually mentioned) the fiftieth anniversary of his death. So the indications are that interest in his work is very much on the increase.

The success of Berners' ballets *The Triumph of Neptune* and *A Wedding Bouquet* was partly a result of the fact that those involved with their creation and production were some of the best-known artistic figures of the time. Unfortunately, it is now impossible to recreate the atmosphere into which these works were born. However, recordings of his five ballets show that the music – which can easily stand on its own – deserves to find a new audience. If the original plots seem a little dated (or, in the case of *Luna Park*, rather politically incorrect) it is to be hoped that new subject matter could be found. Berners' music is so full of character and vitality that this surely must be a possibility. Frederick Ashton used Berners' score from *Luna Park* to create an entirely new production, *Foyer de danse*, in 1932, and more recently, as mentioned above, both *The Triumph of Neptune* and *L'Uomo dai baffi* have undergone the same treatment with success.

Given the renewed interest in Berners' work, a point a little over half a century after his death seems to be an ideal time to reassess his achievements as a composer. Though his output was small, it was self-critically produced and of a consistently high standard. A common theme exploring different states of the human condition is distinguishable in many of his works, and is one which continues to have a relevance for today's society. Berners demonstrated a deep understanding of human nature in his life (his practical jokes often relied on undermining people's predictable reactions to certain situations) as well as his art, and he saw that taking life too seriously could result in tragedy. The fates of Josephine in *A Wedding*

---

[28] Halewood, Lynette. Review at http://www.ballet.co.uk/magazines.
[29] At http://freespace.virgin.net/david.browne/cbl.htm.

Bouquet and the pompous showman from *Luna Park* are examples. Berners suggests that people who have led overly solemn lives – like the statesman and rich aunt from two of the *Trois petites marches funèbres* – are not mourned when they die; pomp and over-inflated egos are worthless and real empathy should be saved for those who deserve it. He admired the simplicity and innocence found in animals (whom he treated anthropomorphically in his music and novels) and in children, but detested the conceit and ostentation which he had had to tolerate in his life as a diplomat and peer.

In addition to this message, Berners' successes in the fields of art, literature and music were, if his autobiographies are to be believed, a triumph over the philistine attitudes of his family and school teachers, and as such are worthy of special commendation. Berners combined a deep-rooted musical understanding with an acute sense of fun and a desire to entertain. With only minimal musical education he earned widespread acclaim from his illustrious contemporaries, and was thoroughly deserving of their praise. A commemoration of Lord Berners would need to include all these aspects of his life and career if it were to provide a fair representation of his achievement. With characteristic succinctness, though, his own epitaph tells us all we really need to know:

Here lies Lord Berners,
One of the learners,
His great love of learning
May earn him a burning
But, praise to the Lord,
He seldom was bored.

Appendix 1

Biography

1883	18 September	Born at Apley Park, Bridgnorth, Shropshire. Only child of Hugh Tyrwhitt and Julia, née Foster. His parents had married in Shropshire on 10 August, 1882.
c1890		Moves with mother to Althrey, near Wrexham, Clwyd.
c1891		Begins lessons with private tutor – the local curate.
c1893		Enrols at Cheam boarding school. He refers to it as Elmley in his autobiography, *First Childhood*.
1894	26 January	Paternal grandfather Sir Henry Tyrwhitt (b.1839) dies at Stanley hall. The title of baronet passes to Gerald's uncle Raymond Tyrwhitt.
1897	Spring	Passes Eton entrance examinations. At Eton he lives in Coleridge House, Keate's Lane, Eton.
c1898		Buys a score of Wagner's *Das Rheingold*.
1899	29 September	Maternal grandfather, William Orme Foster (b.1814), dies aged 85, leaving a fortune of one million pounds.
1900		Finishes at Eton.
		Sent to Normandy at the direction of his parents to learn French in preparation for a career in the diplomatic corps.
1901	January	Goes to Dresden to learn German. While there he sees *Fidelio*, *Carmen*, and *Till Eulenspiegel*.
		Takes orchestration lessons with Edmund Kretschmer.

1904		Travels to Italy for the first time. Visits Lugano, Florence and Sorrento. Spends the next seven years travelling through Europe – not usually staying in one place for longer than three or four months. During this time he regularly attends concerts; amongst the works he hears are *The Magic Flute*, *Martha*, *Salomé*, and *Lohengrin*, as well as works by Debussy.
		Studies with various teachers for the Foreign Office Diplomacy Exams.
1905	December	Writes to his mother telling her that he is not ready to take his diplomacy exams again (by this time he has taken them once and failed).
1906	December	Father, Hugh Tyrwhitt, suddenly taken ill and put into a nursing home.
1907	4 June	His mother records that Gerald had failed his History exam – this is part of the Diplomacy examinations: his second failure.
	26 October	Father, Hon. Hugh Tyrwhitt RN, CVO, CSI, dies suddenly while on the steamship 'Caledonia', en route to Port Said from Marseilles. He had been suffering ill health and the journey had been intended to aid in his convalescence. He is buried at sea.
1908		Julia Tyrwhitt marries Colonel Ward Bennitt.
		Has music lessons with Donald Francis Tovey in London.
1908–9		Goes to Vienna to learn how an embassy is run.
1909		Appointed honorary attaché to the Embassy in Constantinople.
1910	February	Goes back to Vienna to help with the scenery and music for some tableaux vivants.
	March	Visits his mother at her new home,

		Faringdon House, Berkshire.
	May	Goes back to Constantinople via Paris.
1911	December	Sent to Rome as honorary attaché to the embassy there. He is appointed in September, but does not arrive until December. Immediately introduces himself to Stravinsky in Rome.
1913		Begins work on his first mature compositions, *Lieder Album – Three songs in the German Manner*.
1915	May	Writes *Le poisson d'or* which he dedicates to Stravinsky.
		Returns to Rome after studying in Paris.
1916	13 May	Completes his *Trois petites marches funèbres* in Rome.
1917	30 March	First professional performance of his music given by Alfredo Casella who plays the *Trois petites marches funèbres* at the Academia di Santa Cecilia.
		Goes to a performance in Paris of *Le carrosse du Saint-sacrement*, Mérimée's play. Berners is later to write an opera based on the play.
	18 August	Lady Berners, Gerald's paternal grandmother, dies at Ashwellthorpe, Norwich, aged 81. The title passes to her son, Sir Raymond Robert Tyrwhitt-Wilson, who becomes the 13th Baron.
	August	J & W Chester Ltd publish *Trois petites marches funèbres*, completed on 13 May 1916.
1918	15 April	Attends premiere of his puppet ballet *L'Uomo dai baffi*. It is performed by Balli Plastici (a puppet theatre) at the Teatro dei Piccoli di Palazzo Odescalchi, Rome.
	5 September	Lord Berners (Sir Raymond Robert Tyrwhitt-Wilson, 13th Baron) dies in London, aged 63, after holding the title for only one year. On his death the titles of Baron and Baronet pass to Gerald, as Raymond was unmarried and had no children. Gerald becomes the 14th Lord

		Berners, and 5th Baronet.
1919	1 January	Sees in the new year with Diaghilev in London.
	February	Chester publish *Le poisson d'or*.
	8 March	Attends premiere of *Three Pieces for Orchestra* in Manchester, conducted by Eugene Goossens. On 9 January he had written to Stravinsky: 'I am pleased about the performance because, for the moment, Manchester has the best orchestra in England and the conductor will do them very well.'[1]
	June	Quits his job with the Embassy in Rome. Becomes known as Gerald Tyrwhitt-Wilson (Lady Berners' heirs took her maiden name, Wilson, before inheriting; Berners had not anticipated his inheritance and so was a little late in changing his name).
	17 June	Ernest Ansermet conducts the *Three Pieces for Orchestra* for Diaghilev at a concert of English music in Paris, under the patronage of Lord Derby. The concert is repeated on 18 June at the Alhambra in London.
1920	April	Chester publish *Lieder Album – Three Songs in the German Manner*, written 1913–18.
	December	Chester publish *Three English Songs*, written 1920.
1921	January	Chester publish *Trois Chansons*, written 1920.
1921	7 June	First English performance of *The Rite of Spring*. *Fantaisie Espagnole* is performed at the same concert which is held at the Queen's Hall, London, conducted by Eugene Goosens.

---

[1] From a letter from Berners to Stravinsky, Stravinsky, Igor and Craft, Robert: *Memories and Commentaries* (Faber Music LTD, London, 1960, 85).

1923	5 August	*Valses bourgeoises* performed in Salzburg at the second ISCM Festival. Walton's *String Quartet* and Bliss's *Rhapsody* are the only other British contributions. A critic in *The Times* calls Berners' piano duet 'blasés trifles'[2] but they are better received than Walton's quartet. Berners meets Alban Berg and Schoenberg at the Festival
1924	24 April	*Le carrosse du Saint-sacrement*, receives its premiere at the Théâtre des Champs-Elysées, Paris, conducted by Ernest Ansermet.
1925		Meets the young English painter Christopher Wood (1901–30) in Rome. (Wood will design the décor for *Luna Park* in 1930.)
1926	7 November	First concert performance of *Fugue in C minor* takes place at the Royal Albert Hall, London as part of a Sunday afternoon concert. Sir Thomas Beecham conducts the London Symphony Orchestra.
	3 December	First ballet, *The Triumph of Neptune*, written to commission for Diaghilev, receives its premiere at the Lyceum Theatre, London.
1928		Buys a new house, 3 Foro Romano, Rome, which remains in his possession for the next ten years. It cost '£9,000 or more'.[3]
1929		Buys a house in London, 3 Halkin Street, off Belgrave Square.
	June–July	Rex Whistler goes to stay with Berners in Rome.
	19 August	Diaghilev dies in Venice.
	24 October	Suffers losses in the Wall Street Crash, but these are less severe than he makes out.
1930	February	The Camargo Society is formed, aiming to establish a British ballet tradition. Berners joins in December. Frederick Ashton is

---

[2] 'The Salzburg Festival', *The Times*, 14 August 1923, 11.
[3] Amory, 1998, 110.

	choreographer and leading dancer, Constant Lambert the conductor. It is a forerunner of the Sadler's Wells Ballet.
27 March	Second ballet, *Luna Park*, receives its premiere at the London Pavilion. It is written for one of C B Cochran's revues.
1931	Sacheverell Sitwell dedicates his book *Spanish Baroque Art* to Berners. Walton dedicates *Belshazzar's Feast* to Berners 'in return for a badly needed fifty pounds'.[4]
15 February	Mother dies at Faringdon House. Step-father dies five weeks later, on 21 March, at the age of 92. By August 1931 Berners has moved to Faringdon permanently.
c. 9 July	First painting exhibition at the Lefevre Gallery, 1A King Street, St James's, London. Of the 38 paintings on exhibition, Berners sells all but two on the first day, with the prices ranging from £8 to £35, and the average being just under £17.
September	Begins work on the first volume of his autobiography, *First Childhood*. It is not published until 1934.
1932	Meets 20-year-old Robert Heber Percy, during a weekend visit to Michael Duff at Vaynol. Heber Percy is to live with Berners at Faringdon for the last 18 years of Berners' life, and he continues living there until his own death in 1987.
9 October	Premiere of Ashton's ballet, *Foyer de danse* at the Mercury Theatre, Notting Hill, London, at the opening of the Ballet Club's autumn season. This uses Berners' music from *Luna Park*, but set to an entirely different scenario devised by Ashton. It stars Ashton and Alicia Markova.
1932	Meets Salvador and Gala Dali at the

---

[4] Amory, 1998, 200.

		Princesse de Polignac's home in Paris.
1934	February	*First Childhood* published by Constable.
1935		Builds the last traditional folly in England near his home in Faringdon. The architect is Lord Gerald Wellesley, later the seventh Duke of Wellington. (Berners provides the wording for the notice at the entrance himself: 'Members of the Public committing suicide from this tower do so at their own risk'. The octagonal tower stands nearly one hundred feet tall.)
1936	1 March	Completes *The Camel* (novel) which he begins in mid-January and dedicates to the Betjemans. It is published by Constable and is well received.
	27 April	Third ballet, *A Wedding Bouquet*, is premiered at Sadler's Wells, London. Berners designs the sets and costumes himself.
	May	Holds his second successful exhibition of oil paintings at the Lefevre Gallery, London.
1937		*The Girls of Radcliff Hall* (novel) is published privately because of its risqué content.
1939	27 April	Fourth ballet, *Cupid and Psyche*, is premiered at Sadler's Wells, London. It is a total flop and lasts for only five performances.
1939	September–October	Has a nervous breakdown as a result of depression caused by the onset of World War II. Goes to Oxford to stay with Maurice Bowra at Wadham College and then moves into other lodgings in Oxford. Whilst there he works at the Taylorian Institute where he is employed to catalogue foreign books. Bowra secures him this post.
1939	November	Begins to visit Faringdon at weekends, eventually moving back there permanently.
1941	Summer	Heber Percy returns to Faringdon from the Middle East where he had been doing

		intelligence work. He is granted leave on medical grounds.
1941	July	Two novels, *Far from the Madding War* and *Count Omega* are published by Constable.
1941	August ?	*Percy Wallingford* and *Mr Pidger* (two short novels) are published together in one volume by Blackwell.
1942	Spring	*The Romance of a Nose* (novel) is published by Constable.
	June	A play, *The Furies*, written by Berners is staged at the Oxford Playhouse, it runs for one week. Designs are by Tanya Moiseiwitch. It receives encouraging reviews but is not afterwards staged in London as Berners hoped it might be.
	11 July	Heber Percy marries Jennifer Fry. They are to divorce in 1948. (There is one daughter from the marriage, Victoria Gala, born 28 February 1943.)
1943	Before April	Composes a complete score for the Ealing film *The Halfway House*. The film opens on 14 April, 1944.
1944		Provides two numbers for the Ealing film *Champagne Charlie*.
1945	July	*A Distant Prospect* (second volume of autobiography) is published by Constable.
	December	*The Expulsion from Paradise* is premiered as part of the incidental music to a pantomime organised by Penelope Betjeman. The pantomime is staged at Farnborough Parish Church, Hampshire.
1946	12 November	Fifth ballet, *Les Sirènes*, is premiered at the Royal Opera House, Covent Garden.
1947		Finishes his second complete film score, for the Ealing production *Nicholas Nickleby*.
1949	12 October	*A Wedding Bouquet* is first performed in America by the Sadler's Wells Ballet at the

		Metropolitan Opera House, New York.
1950	19 April	Dies 'of bad heart and blood pressure'[5] at Faringdon House aged 66 leaving an estate worth £214, 306.
1950	22 April	Funeral takes place. Berners is cremated at Oxford crematorium.

[5] Heber Percy quoted in Amory, 1998, 234.

Appendix 2

The Musical Works of
Lord Berners

This list of works gives the following information: date and place (if known) of composition in column 1. Then, in column 2: title, description and author of text (if applicable); description of the music, including instrumentation; dedication (if applicable); present location and details of the manuscripts (GB-Lbl is the British Library, London. GB-Far is Faringdon House, Faringdon, Oxfordshire (formerly in Berkshire); publication details of the music; details of the first performance (where known).

Abbreviations

accomp.	accompaniment	MS, MSS	manuscript,
arr.	arranged,		manuscripts
	arrangement	mvts	movements
bn	bassoon	ob	oboe
bs cl	bass clarinet	orch.	orchestra,
cl	clarinet		orchestrated
cond.	conductor,	org	organ
	conducted by	orig.	originally
contra bn	contra bassoon	perc	percussion
cor ang	cor anglais	perfd	performed
crt	cornet	pf	pianoforte
ded.	dedication,	picc	piccolo
	dedicated to	prem.	premiere
eng hn	English horn	pubn	publication
fl	flute	str	strings
hn	horn	tb	trombone
hp	harp	tpt	trumpet
inst.	instrumental	unpubd	unpublished

c.1897–1900   **An Egyptian Princess**

text: Berners

music: A musical play in two acts. 13 numbers – 7 solos, 4 choruses, 1 duet and 1 trio.

Unpubd

1913–18   **Lieder Album: Three songs in the German manner**

text: Heine, H, Buch der Lieder, 1827. Poems XLVII, XLV and XXXVII in *Der Heimkehr*

music: 3 songs with pf accomp.
     1. *Du bist wie eine Blume*
     2. *König Wiswamitra*
     3. *Weihnachtslied*

MSS: GB-Lbl, 8 pp.

pubn: J & W Chester Ltd, April 1920. (500 copies ordered by Berners). Price 3s. 0d.

c.1914/15   **Dispute entre le papillon et le crapaud**

music: piece for pf

MSS: autograph MS was GB-Far (unsigned), now unknown[1]

pubn: Chester Music Ltd, 1980

May 1915,   **Le poisson d'or**
Rome

text: Berners (introductory poem)

music: piece for pf

ded.:   'à Igor Stravinsky'

MSS: GB-Lbl

pubn: J & W Chester Ltd, February 1919. (1000 copies ordered by Berners in February under the title: *Le poisson d'or, Poème et Musique de Lord Berners*). Price 3s. 0d. The front cover, frontispiece and vignette were specially created by Natalia Gontcharowa

---

[1] All of Berners' manuscripts were moved from the Faringdon estate to the British Library in the 1990s. The score for this work seems to have been lost in transition.

13 May 1916,   **Trois petites marches funèbres**[2]
Rome   music: 3 pieces for pf, later orch.
                          1. *Pour un homme d'état*
                          2. *Pour un canari*
                          3. *Pour une tante à l'héritage*
                MSS: autograph MS GB-Lbl, 10 pp.
                pubn: Gaetano e Paolo Luigi Mignani, Firenze. First
                          English edition published by J & W Chester Ltd,
                          August, 1917. (1000 copies ordered by Berners).
                          First pubd under the name Gerald Tyrwhitt, price
                          2s. 6d
                prem: 30 March 1917, Academia Santa Cecilia, Alfredo
                          Casella (pf). This was Berners' first professional
                          performance. The orchestrated versions were used
                          for dances in both Rome and Berlin, before
                          Penelope Spencer danced one of them ('Death Of
                          A Rich Aunt') in London in 1926 and 1928

1917   **Fragments psychologiques**[3]
                music: 3 pieces for pf
                          1. *La haine*
                          2. *Le rire*
                          3. *Un soupir*
                MSS: Autograph MS GB-Lbl, 11pp. in ink
                pubn: J & W Chester Ltd, January 1919, under name
                          Gerald Tyrwhitt (300 copies ordered by Berners).
                          Price 3s. 0d

1917   **Valses bourgeoises**
                music: 3 pieces for pf duet (4 hands)
                          1. *Valse brillante*
                          2. *Valse caprice*
                          3. *Strauss, Strauss et Straus*
                pubn: J & W Chester Ltd, 1919, price 7s 6d
                prem: 5 August 1923 as part of a concert given at the
                          International Festival of Contemporary Music,
                          Salzburg

---

[2] Instrumental version, arranged by Casella, appeared in the puppet ballet *L'Uomo dai baffi*.
[3] Also used in *L'Uomo dai baffi*.

1917   **Trois morceaux**

music: 3 pieces for pf duet. Arr. for orch. (1917) under the title *Three Pieces for Orchestra*:

1. *Chinoiserie*
2. *Valse sentimentale*
3. *Kasatchok*

ded.:   1. 'à Michel Larionow'
2. 'à Eugène Goossens'
3. 'à Natalia Gontcharowa'

MSS: GB-Lbl (full score); GB-Lbl (pf duet score)

pubn: J & W Chester Ltd, 1919 (pf duet. Price 6s. 0d) 'Couverture, Illustrations et Ornement de Michel Larionow'; J & W Chester Ltd, 1921 (orch. version). Price: full score 20s. 0d

prem: Orch. version 8 March 1919, Manchester, Hallé Concerts Society. Cond. Eugene Goossens

1918   **Portsmouth Point**[4]

text: after an etching by Rowlandson (1756–1827)

music: orig. planned as a ballet, but first written as a piece for pf. Berners completed only 50 bars of an orch. arr. before abandoning the work

MSS: GB-Lbl

unpubd

prem: 15 April, 1918 (inst. version in *L'Uomo dai baffi*)

1918   **L'Uomo dai baffi**

music: Puppet ballet. Arr. by Casella for fl, ob, cl in A, bn, pf, 5 str.

7 mvts:

1. *The Golden Road* (arr. of 'Le rire')
2. *Intermezzo* (arr. of 'Un soupir')
3. *The Blue Ballerina* (arr. of 'Pour un homme d'état')
4. *The Drunken Dancer* (arr. of 'Pour un canari')
5. *The Tip-Toeing White Mice* (arr. of 'Pour une tante à l'héritage')

---

[4] Also used in *L'Uomo dai baffi*.

6. *Intermezzo* (arr. of 'La haine')
7. *It's Raining Cigarettes* (arr. of Portsmouth Point)

MSS: GB-Lbl (photocopy of autograph MS), 35 pp.
pubn: see prem below
prem: 15 April 1918. Performed by Balli Plastici (a puppet theatre) at the Teatro dei Piccoli di Palazzo Odescalchi, Rome. (Included as part of a performance organised by Fortunato Depero for the Compagnia Marionettistica of Gorno dell'Acqua)

1918
(Faringdon)
Orch. Rome,
1919

Fantaisie espagnole

music: piece for orch. for picc, 3 fl, 2 ob, eng hn, 3 cl, bs cl, 3 bn, contrabn, 4 hn, 3 tpt, 3 tb, tuba, timps, perc, 2 hps, str. Later arr. for pf duet
1. *Prélude*
2. *Fandango*
3. *Pasodoblé*
ded.: 'G. Francesco Malipiero'
MSS: GB-Lbl (full score 47 pp.); GB-Lbl (pf duet score)
pubn: J & W Chester Ltd, 1920 (orch. version). Prices: full score 20s. 0d, miniature score 4s. 0d. J & W Chester Ltd, 1920–21 (pf duet, price 6s. 0d)
prem: 24 September, 1919, Queen's Hall, New Queen's Hall Orchestra, conducted by Sir Henry J Wood; also orch. version perfd 7 June 1921 in the same concert as the first English concert perf. of Stravinsky's *The Rite of Spring*, at the Queen's Hall, London, conducted by Eugene Goossens

1920

Trois chansons

texts: Georges Jean-Aubry (possibly unpubd)
music: 3 songs with pf accomp.
1. *Romance*
2. *L'étoile filante*
3. *La fiancée du timbalier*
MSS: Pencil sketch GB-Lbl (No. 3 only)

pubn: J & W Chester Ltd, January 1921. (500 copies ordered by Berners). Price 3s. 0d

1920   **Three Songs**

texts: No.1 and No.3 from *A Sailor's Garland*, selected and edited by John Masefield in 1906. No.2 John Masefield. Appeared in *A Broad Sheet*, No.19, July 1903, published by Elkin and Matthews

music: 3 songs with pf accomp.
1.   *The Rio Grande (Capstan Shanty)*
2.   *Theodore or The Pirate King*
3.   *A Long Time Ago (Halliards Chanty)*

MSS: autograph MS GB-Lbl

pubn: J & W Chester Ltd, December 1920. (500 copies ordered by Berners). Price 3s. 0d. Orig. titled, *Three Songs in the English Manner*

1920   **Three English Songs**

text: No.1 Thomas Dekker (from the play *Patient Grissel*). No.2 Robert Graves. No.3 Esther Lilian Duff.

Music: 1. *Lullaby*
2. *Lady Visitor in the Pauper Ward*
3. *The Green-eyed Monster*

MSS: autograph MS in ink with editorial annotations GB-Lbl, 7 pp.

pubn: J & W Chester Ltd, 1921. Price 3s. 0d

1921   **Dialogue between Tom Filuter and his man, by Ned the dog stealer**

text: "'The Dialogue between Tom Flinter and his Man, by Ned the Dog Stealer' appeared in *A Broad Sheet*, No. 3, March 1902, published by Elkin and Matthews. Lord Berners' rendering of the name in all sources and contracts as Filuter, not Flinter, could be a double entendre. (*Filouter* in French, is to steal or swindle)" [5]

music: song with pf accomp.

---

[5] Dickinson, P, 'Editorial notes' in *Lord Berners The Collected Vocal Music*, 1979, 47.

MSS: autograph MS GB-Lbl, 4 pp.
pubn: J & W Chester Ltd, April 1924. (500 copies ordered by Berners). Price 2s. 0d

1920 – 22   **Le carrosse du Saint-sacrement**
(revised 1923) text: Berners wrote his own libretto based on the play by Prosper Mérimée, 1828

music: Comic opera in 1 act. Scored for 2 fl, 2 ob, cor ang., 2 cl in B-flat, 2 bn, contra bn, 2 hn, 2 tpt, 2 tb, perc, pf, hp, 5 str
Cast:

The Viceroy	Baritone
Martinez, the Viceroy's private secretary	Tenor
Balthasar, the Viceroy's valet	Tenor
La Périchole, the Viceroy's mistress	Mezzo-Soprano
Thomas, the Minister	Bass
The Bishop of Lima	Bass
The Canon	Tenor

ded.:   'To my travelling companions in Italy. Perugia – Rome, Summer, 1920.'
MSS: GB-Lbl (full score)
pubn: J & W Chester Ltd, 1923, rev. 1926. Vocal score price 20s. 0d
prem: 24 April 1924, Théâtre des Champs-Elysées, Paris. Performance also included Stravinsky's *L'histoire du soldat* and *La chatte*, a ballet by Henri Sauguet. Some of the interlude music was later arranged as an orchestral work, *Caprice péruvien*, by Berners and Constant Lambert

May 1924, **Fugue in C minor**
Paris   music: Short orchestral piece scored for 3 fl, picc, 2 ob, 2 cl in B-flat, contra bn, 4 hn, 2 tpt, 2 tb, perc, org (ad lib), hp, 5 str
ded.:   'Princess Edmond de Polignac'
MSS: autograph MS in pencil with editorial annotations, GB-Lbl, 57 pp.

pubn: J & W Chester Ltd, 1928. Prices: full score 30s. 0d., miniature score 4s. 0d

prem: 1926 His Majesty's Theatre, London, as symphonic interlude between ballets, conducted by Eugene Goossens. First concert performance 7 November 1926 at the Royal Albert Hall, London, London Symphony Orchestra cond. Sir Thomas Beecham. It was performed as part of a Sunday afternoon concert series

1926   The Triumph of Neptune

text: scenario by Sacheverell Sitwell

music: ballet in ten tableaux (orig. twelve) for Diaghilev's Ballets Russes. Contents:
Prelude
Scene I: London Bridge, Schottische, Fanfare
Scene II: Cloudland, Fanfare
Scene III: Farewell
Scene IV: Shipwreck
Scene V: The Frozen Forest, Variations, Coda
Scene VI: Dance of Britannia, Entr'acte (Hornpipe)
Scene VII: The Sailor's Return, Polka
Scene VIII: Sunday Morning (Intermezzo), Fanfare
Scene IX: The Triumph of Neptune, Finale, Dance of the Fairy Princess, Harlequinade, Variation, Hornpipe
Scene X: Apotheosis
Scored for 3 fl, picc, 2 ob, cor ang, 2 cl in B-flat, 2 bn, contra bn, 4 hn, crt in B-flat, 3 tpt, 2 tb, bass tb, tuba, timps, perc, 5 str, pf, hrp
A suite was also arranged, which consisted of nine numbers from the original score. The order of the numbers was completely changed, and appear as follows:
1. Harlequinade
2. Dance of the Fairy Princess
3. Schottische

4. Cloudland
5. Intermezzo: Sunday Morning
6. Polka
7. Hornpipe
8. The Frozen Forest
9. Apotheosis

Ded.:   'To Viscount Rothermere. London. December, 1926'

MSS: autograph MS GB-Lbl

pubn: J & W Chester Ltd, 1926 (orch. score). J & W Chester Ltd, 1927 (complete pf score), price 12s. 0d. J & W Chester Ltd, 1927, three extracts for pf: *Hornpipe* (price 2s. 0d.), *Pantomime* and *Intermezzo* (price 2s. 0d). J & W Chester Ltd, 1975 (Suite for pf, 12pp.) J & W Chester Ltd, 1984 (Suite arr. for symphonic wind band by Bram Wiggins, 51pp.)

prem: 3 December 1926, Lyceum, London. Choreography by Georges Balanchine. Cond. Henri Defosse

Cast:

The Fairy Queen	Mlle. Alexandra Danilova
Tom Tug	M. Serge Lifar
W Brown, a journalist	M. Michael Fedorov
Britannia	Mme. Lydia Sokolova
Emerald	Mme. Lubov Tchernicheva
Ruby	Mme. Vera Petrova
Cupid	M. Stanislav Idzikowsky

The Fairies   Mmes. Savina, Maikerska, Soumarokova, Markova, Istomina, Vadimova, Branitska, Orlova, Slavinsa, Klemetska, Zarina, Obidennaia, Evina, Miklachevska, Jasevitch, Kouchpetovska

Sylphs	Mme. Lubov Tchernicheva
	Mme. Vera Petrova
Street Dancer	Mlle. Tatiana Chamie
The Sailor's Wife	Mlle. Barash
The Sailor's Mother	Mlle. Fedorova
Snowball, a black man	M. Georges Balanchine

Harlequins   MM. Leon Woizikovsky, Nicholas Efimov, Constantin Tcherkas, Nicolas Kremev, Richard Domansky

Pages   MM. Thadée Slavinsky, Jazinsky, Fedorov, Kochanovsky, Lissanevitch, Romov, Borovsky, Strchnev, Gaubier

Dandy   M. Constantin Tcherkas

Journalists   MM. Jazinsky, Vinter

Policemen   MM. Hoyer, Cieplinsky

Cab Driver   M. Pavlov

Telescope Keepers   MM. Borovsky, Petrakevitch

Waiter   M. Lissanevitch

Beggar   M. Georges Balanchine

Street Hawkers   MM. Romov, Ladre

Workmen   MM. Strechnev, Ignatov, Hoyer II

Newsvendors   MM. Jazinsky, Vinter

Newspaper Boys   MM. Strechnev, Hoyer II, Ignatov

Officer   M. Domansky

Chimney Sweep   M. Gaubier

King of the Ogres   M. Michael Pavlov

Ogres   MM. Efimov, Romov, Kochanovsky, Borovsky, Ladre, Gaubier, Mmes. Chamie, Fedorova, Barash, Matveeva

Clowns   MM. Petrakevitch, Ladre

Neptune's Attendants   MM. Vinter, Ignatov, Hoyer II, Michaelov

Voice   M. Enrico Garcia

'Scenery and costumes by George and Robert Cruikshank, Tofts, Honigold and Webb, collected by Mr B Pollock and Mr H J Webb, adapted and executed by Prince A Shervachidze.'

The Triumph of Neptune received its first concert performance at a Proms concert on 19 September 1929 and was newly worked by David Bintley as *Punch and the Street Party* in 1979 for Sadler's Wells Royal Ballet

1930 **Luna Park**

text: scenario by Boris Kochno

music: 'Fantastic Ballet in One Act'. Scored for fl/picc, ob/cor ang., cl in B-flat, bn, 2 hn, 2 tpt, tb, perc, hrp, str.

Written for C B Cochran's 1930 Revue.

ded. 'Dedicated to Charles B Cochran, London March, 1930'

MSS: GB-Lbl autograph pf score; GB-Lbl full score – copy with autograph annotations

pubn: J & W Chester Ltd, 1930. J & W Chester Ltd, also published a piano score, 1930, price 5s. 0d, and an orchestral suite

prem: Thursday 27 March 1930, London Pavilion, London. Choreography by Balanchine; décor and costumes by Christopher Wood. Cond. Charles Prentice. Produced by C B Cochran

Cast:

The Showman	M. Nicolas Efimov
The Man with Three Heads	
	M. Constantin Tcherkas
The Three-legged Juggler	
	M. Richard Domansky
The One-legged Ballerina	Mlle. Alice Nikitina
The Man with Six Arms	M. Serge Lifar

A concert performance of *Luna Park* was given by the BBC Symphony Orchestra at a Proms concert on 19 September 1931, conducted by Sir Henry J Wood. The score was re-used by Frederick Ashton for his 1932 ballet *Foyer de danse* (see Chapter 6: The Ballets). This was premiered in October 1932 at the Mercury Theatre, London

c.1930 **Choral Prelude on 'In Dulci Jubilo'**

music: Arr. of Bach's *In Dulci Jubilo* (Chorale Prelude BWV 729) by Berners for *A Bach Book for*

Harriet Cohen, twelve transcriptions of Bach pieces by various British composers for pf

ded.: 'For Harriet Cohen'

pubn: Oxford University Press, 1932

1931 **Fanfare**

music: Short piece (less than one minute) for tpts, tbs and perc written for the annual St Cecilia's Day concert in aid of the Musicians Benevolent Fund.

prem: 1931

April 1936
London

A Wedding Bouquet

text: Gertrude Stein, *They must. Be wedded. To their wife.* Adapted by Berners

music: one act comic ballet with chorus. Scored for 2 fl, picc, 2 ob, 2 cl in B-flat, bn, 4 hn, 2 tpt, 3 tb, timps, perc, hrp, 5 str, voices (SATB)

ded.: 'To LILIAN BAYLIS C.H.; M.A.OXON. (Hon); LL.D. (BIRM.) London April, 1936'

MSS: autograph MS, GB-Lbl. A typescript of the synopsis is inserted, dated 15 Dec 1937

pubn: J & W Chester Ltd, 1936. J & W Chester Ltd, 1938 (pf including text) price 12s. 0d

prem: 27 April 1937, London, Sadler's Wells. Cond. Constant Lambert; choreography by Frederick Ashton; settings and costumes designed by Berners and made under the supervision of William Chappell.

Cast:

Webster	Ninette de Valois
	afterwards Sheila McCarthy
Two Peasant Girls	Linda Sheridan, Joan Leaman
Two Peasant Boys	Paul Reymond, Alan Carter
Josephine	June Brae
Paul	Harold Turner
John	William Chappell
Violet	Pamela May
Ernest	Claude Newman
Thérèse	Elizabeth Miller

Julia	Margot Fonteyn
Bridegroom	Robert Helpmann
Pépé (Julia's Dog)	Julia Farron
Arthur	Leslie Edwards
Guy	Michael Somes
Four Guests	Gwyneth Mathews,

Wenda Horsburgh, Joy Newton, Anne Spicer

Two Gendarmes	Paul Reymond, Alan Carter
Bride	Mary Honer
Bridesmaids	Molly Brown, Jill Gregory

Members of the Opera Company
Misses Teychenne, Jackson, Strudwick, Carline,
Lewtas, Tollworthy. Messrs. Tree, Mossop,
Cannon, Barber.

First performed in the United States by the
Sadler's Wells Ballet at the Metropolitan Opera
House, New York, 25 October 1949. This
performance starred Margaret Dale as the Bride,
Robert Helpmann as the Bridegroom, Moira
Shearer as Julia, June Brae as Josephine, Pauline
Clayden as Pépé, and Palma Nye as Webster. For
the New York performances a narrator, Constant
Lambert, replaced the chorus. *A Wedding
Bouquet* was chosen for the Sadler's Wells
twenty-first anniversary gala in 1951 at the
Sadler's Wells Theatre, London, on 15 May. At
this performance Ninette de Valois, the director
of the ballet company, repeated her role as
Webster, the maid, and Constant Lambert was
again used as narrator. The ballet was also
performed at the Lillian Baylis centenary evening
in 1974

1938–39   **Cupid and Psyche**
music: ballet in 3 scenes
unpubd
prem: 27 April 1939, Sadler's Wells, London. Cond.
         Constant Lambert

Cast:

Pan	Michael Somes
Nymph	Palma Nye, Joan Leaman
Psyche	Julia Farron
Cupid	Frank Staff
Venus	June Brae
Psyche's Sisters	Mary Honer, Elizabeth Miller
Ceres	Margot Fonteyn*
Minerva	Mary Honer
Diana	Elizabeth Miller
Appollo	Richard Ellis
Juno	Ursula Moreton
Jupiter	David Grey
Narrators	Kathleen Hilditch, Margaret Tepler

Tanagra Women, Townspeople, Attendants on Venus, Zelphyrs, Attendants on Minerva, Attendants on Diana, Attendants on Juno and Jupiter: Corps de ballet

* Standing in for Pamela May who was ill

Sets and costumes designed by Sir Francis Rose at Berners' request and made by Mme. Ira Belline. Choreography was by Frederick Ashton.

c.1940 **Red Roses and Red Noses**

text: Lord Berners

music: song with pf accomp.

ded.: 'To a young lady who expressed the wish that, when she died, red roses might be strewn upon her tomb'

MSS: Composer's MS GB-Lbl
Ink copy in the possession of Sir Alfred Beit

pubn: Chester Music Ltd, 1980

1941, **Polka**
Oxford

music: piece for pf, it also appeared in the film Champagne Charlie, arr. by Ernest Irving, Musical director of Ealing Studios

MSS: Composer's MS GB-Lbl

pubn: Chester Music Ltd, 1980

prem: 29 December 1941, Radcliffe Infirmary, Oxford. Perf. by Tom Bell and Lionel Grunbaum (two pianos) in a pantomime called *Cinderella or There's Many a Slipper*. The film was first shown on 25 August 1945

1943   **Valse**
music: pf solo. The first 213 bars of the piece were used in the film *The Halfway House* as background music to a séance scene. The film opened on 14 April 1944
MSS: composer's MS GB- Lbl, headed 'Valse (to be played during the séance)'
pubn: Chester Music Ltd, 1980

1943   **The Halfway House**
music: Film score. *The Halfway House*, an Ealing Studios production, was directed by Basil Dearden and starred Glynis Johns and Guy Middleton
unpubd
prem: the film opened on 14 April 1944

1943   **Come on Algernon**
text: T E B Clarke
music: song written for the soundtrack for the film *Champagne Charlie*, first shown on 25 August 1944
MSS: Ink copy in the possession of Una Bart, Music Director at Ealing studios at the time when the song was written
pubn: Chester Music Ltd, 1980

1943–44   **Champagne Charlie**
music: 2 numbers for film score: *Come on Algernon* (song) and *Polka* (pf). See above

c.1945   **March**
music: piece for solo pf, later scored for brass (a semitone lower) by Philip Lane
pubn: Chester Music Ltd, 1980

24 November   **The Expulsion from Paradise**
1945
music: piece for solo pf, written for Penelope Betjeman to accompany a nativity play at Farnborough Parish Church that was organised by her. It was played on a harmonium
ded.:   'for Penelope Betjeman'
MSS: composer's MS in the possession of Penelope Betjeman
pubn: Chester Music Ltd, 1980
prem: December 1945

July 1946   **Les Sirènes** (orig. title to be *Seagulls,* it then became *Sirens and Seagulls* before finally being changed to *Les Sirènes*)
music: ballet, set on the Riviera at the turn of the century. Scored for 2 fl, picc, 2 ob, 2 cl in B-flat, 2bn, 4 hn, 2 tpt, 3 tb, tba (ad lib), timps, 2 (or 3) perc, pf (ad lib), celeste (ad lib), hrp, 5 str
MSS: GB-Lbl, (part 1, 119pp)
unpubd
prem: 12 November 1946, the Royal Opera House, Covent Garden.
Cast:

La Bolero	Margot Fonteyn
Her Chauffeur-Accompanist	Leslie Edwards
King Hihat of Agpar	Frederick Ashton
Adelino Canberra (of the Adelaide opera)	Robert Helpmann
Mermaids	Palma Nye, Gillian Lyne
Seagulls	Margaret Dale, Alexis Rassine
Children	Pauline Clayden, Alexander Grant, Guinevere Parry, Mavis Spence
Nannies	Anne Gieves, Fiorella Keane
Gendarmes	Paul Reymond, Alec Martin

Flowerwoman	Betty Cooper
Countess Kitty	Beryl Grey
Captain Bay Vavasour	Michael Somes
The Smart Set, King Hihat's Suite	Corps de ballet

Choreography was by Frederick Ashton and the designs were by Cecil Beaton. The ballet ran for nineteen performances, after which it was never revived

1947   **Nicholas Nickleby**
music: film score
ded.:   'Dedicated to Ernest Irving'
MSS: GB-Lbl, autograph pf score, 11 pp., and sketches; GB-Lbl autograph MS of the orchestration by Ernest Irving
pubn: Chappell, 1947

Appendix 3

The Literary Works of
Lord Berners

1931–34   **First Childhood**
text: first volume of autobiography
ded: 'To Robert Heber Percy Whose Knowledge of Orthography And Literary Style Has Proved Invaluable'
pubn: Constable, 1934, London, 255pp.

1936   **The Camel**
text: short novel
ded: 'To John and Penelope Betjeman'
pubn: London, Constable, 1936, 175pp., with three illustrations by Berners

1937   **The Girls of Radcliff Hall**
text: short novel
pubn: privately published under the pseudonym Adela Quebec, c. 1937, 100pp.

1941   **Far from the Madding War**
text: short novel
ded: 'To David and Rachel Cecil'
pubn: London, Constable, 1941, 193pp., with three illustrations by Berners

1941   **Count Omega**
text: short novel
ded: 'To Rosamund Lehman'
pubn: London, Constable, 1941, 208pp., with a frontispiece by Berners

1941   **Percy Wallingford** and **Mr Pidger**
text: Two short novels

pubn: Oxford, Blackwell, 1941, 105pp.

1941   **The Romance of a Nose**
              text: short novel
              pubn: London, Constable, 1941, (though issuing was
                       delayed until 1942) 201pp., with a frontispiece by
                       Berners

1945   **A Distant Prospect**
              text: second volume of autobiography
              pubn: London, Constable, 1945, 125pp.

c.1949–50   **The Château de Résenlieu**
              text: third volume of autobiography, left unfinished at
                       time of death
              pubn: Canada, Turtle Point Press and Helen Marx Books,
                       2000, 84pp.

Appendix 4

Discography

Since 1994 all of Berners' works have been issued on CD. This is not a complete discography but a list of the most significant CD releases. LP recordings can still be obtained from archives.

English Music for Piano Duet (Berners, Lambert, Rawsthorne, Walton, Lane), Albany Records, Troy 142, recorded

Lord Berners 1883–1950 (a collection), Symposium, 1278, issued 2000

Lord Berners: Ballet Music, *Les Sirènes*, *Cupid and Psyche*, *Caprice péruvien*, Marco Polo, 8.223780, recorded 1994, 1995, issued 1995

Lord Berners: *Le carrosse du Saint-sacrement, Caprice péruvien, Fanfare*, Marco Polo, 'CD Marco Polo, 8.225155, recorded 1983, 1995, 1999, issued 2000

Lord Berners: The Complete Vocal and Solo Piano Works, Albany Records, Troy 290, recorded 1994, 1996, issued 1997

Lord Berners: *Songs, Piano Music*, Marco Polo 8.225159, recorded 1998, issued 2000

Lord Berners: *The Triumph of Neptune, L'Uomo dai baffi, Valses bourgeoises, Polka*, Marco Polo 8.223711, recorded 1996, issued 1998

Lord Berners: *The Triumph of Neptune* (Suite), *Nicholas Nickleby incidental music, Trois Morceaux, Fantaisie espagnole*, EMI, 1986, issued 1994

Lord Berners: *Wedding Bouquet, Luna Park, March*, Marco Polo, 8.223716, recorded 1994, issued 1996

Postscript

Since completing the text I have acquired a letter written by Berners from Faringdon House, dated 16 June 1948, to Major Piercy, which includes a particularly poignant comment (in an earlier letter from Berners, dated 23 August 1943, it is clear that Major Piercy had offered the assistance of the RAF Orchestra and the services of copyists):

> Dear Major Piercy
>
> Thank you very much for your letter.
>
> Alas! For the last year I have been ill and I am still not well enough to write any music. But, if by a happy miracle I am able to do so, of course I will apply to you.
>
> Yours sincerely
>
> Berners

Sadly for him, and for us, the happy miracle was not to be.

Bibliography

Books

Acton, Harold	*Preface* to *Far from the Madding War* (novel by Berners) (Oxford, Oxford University Press, 1983)
Amory, Mark	*Lord Berners: The Last Eccentric* (London, Chatto and Windus, 1998)
Anon.	*Miniature Essays: Lord Berners* (London, J & W Chester Ltd, 1923)[1]
Balanchine, G and Mason, F	*Balanchine's Festival of Ballet* (London, W H Allen, 1978)
Berners, Lord	*First Childhood* (London, Constable & Co Ltd, 1934)
Berners, Lord	*A Distant Prospect* (London, Constable & Co Ltd, 1945. Reissued by Turtle Point Press and Helen Marx Books, Canada, 1998)
Berners, Lord	*The Château de Résenlieu* (Canada, Turtle Point Press and Helen Marx Books, 2000)
Bland, Alexander	*The Royal Ballet: The First Fifty Years* (London, Threshold, 1981)
Blom, Eric	*Music in England* (Middlesex, Pelican Books, 1942, rev. ed., 1947)
Buckle, Richard	*Diaghilev* (London, Weidenfeld and Nicolson, 1979)
Casella, Alfredo	*The Evolution of Music throughout the history of the Perfect Cadence* (London, J & W Chester Ltd, 1924)
Casella, Alfredo	*Music in My Time* Translated and edited by Spencer Norton (Oklahoma, University of Oklahoma Press, 1955), pp.143–144
Cox, David	*The Henry Woods Proms* (London, BBC, 1980)

---

[1] This is one of a series of books published by Chester between 1921 and 1926 which examined the works of contemporary composers. Bantock, Bax, Holbrooke, Goosens, Moeran and Malipiero are just a few of the composers included. None of the books names the author!

Craft, Robert (ed.)   'Correspondence with Gerald Tyrwhitt' in *Stravinsky Selected Correspondence Volume Two* (London, Faber and Faber, 1984), pp.135–159

Garafola, Lynn   *Diaghilev's Ballets Russes* (Oxford and New York, Oxford University Press, 1989)

Girouard, Mary   'Lord Berners. Artist, Author, Musician and Wit' in *The British Eccentric*, ed. Harriet Bridgeman and Elizabeth Drury (London, Michael Joseph, 1975)

Grigoriev, Serge   *The Diaghilev Ballet 1909–1929*. Translated by Vera Bowen (London, Constable, 1953)

Kavanagh, Julie   *Secret Muses, The Life of Frederick Ashton* (London, Faber and Faber, 1996)

Lambert, Constant   *Music Ho!* (London, Faber and Faber, 1934)

Mosley, Diana   'Lord Berners' in *Loved Ones, Pen Portraits* (London, Sidgwick & Jackson 1985, pp.96–131)

Shead, Richard   *Constant Lambert* (London, Simon Publications, 1973)

Sitwell, Osbert   *Laughter in the Next Room* (London, The Reprint Society, 1950), pp.177–179

Van Den Toorn, P C: *The Music of Igor Stravinsky* (New Haven and London, Yale University Press, 1983)

Vaughan, David   *Frederick Ashton and His Ballets* (London, Adam and Charles Black, 1977)

Vickers, Hugo   *Cecil Beaton* (London, Weidenfeld & Nicolson, 1985. Revised edition 1993)

Westrup, J A   'Lord Berners' in *British Music of our Time* (Middlesex, Pelican Books, 1946)

Woodcock, S C   *The Sadler's Wells Royal Ballet* (London, Sinclair-Stevenson, 1981)

Magazine Articles

Chipchase, Paul   'Record Review: Berners, The Triumph of Neptune…' in *Tempo* clx, (1987), pp.49–50

Crichton, Ronald   'Berners, (Sir Gerald, Hugh Tyrwhitt-Wilson, Baronet)': entry in *The New Groves Dictionary of Music and Musicians* (London, McMillan Publishing, 1980)

Dickinson, Peter   'Lord Berners, 1883–1950 A British avant gardist at the time of World War I' in *Musical Times*, cxxiv, (1983), pp.669–672

Evans, Edwin	'Opera and Lord Berners' in *Musical Times*, lxiv (1923), pp.533–537
Goodwin, Noel	'The Berners Bouquet' in *Dance & Dancers*, cdvii (1983), pp.24–26
Hurd, Michael	'The Centenary of Berners' in *The Times Literary Supplement*, 1983, No.4202, p.1124
Hutchings, Arthur	'Reviews of Music: Lord Berners, The Collected Music for Solo Piano; The Collected Vocal Music', ed. Peter Dickinson in *Music and Letters*, 1983, lxiv/3–4, pp.291–293
Mellers, Wilfred	'Visionary Gleams' in *The Musical Times*, cxxxvii (1996), pp.17–19
Steyn, Mark	'Berners at the Ballet: A Centennial for Gerald Hugh Tyrwhitt Wilson' in *Dancing Times*, lxxiv (1983), pp.31–33
Steyn, Mark	'Lord Berners As A Painter' in *Apollo – the International Magazine of the Arts*, cxx, (1984) pp.128–31

Sleeve Notes, CD Liner Notes and Editorial Notes

Dickinson, Peter	'Sleeve Notes', *A Portrait of Lord Berners (1883–1950) Songs and Piano Music* (Unicorn Records, 1978)
Dickinson, Peter	'Editorial Notes' in *Lord Berners: The Collected Vocal Music* (London, Chester Music, 1980)
Dickinson, Peter	'Editorial Notes' in *Lord Berners: the Collected Music for Solo Piano* (London, Chester Music, 1980)
Dickinson, Peter	'Sleeve Notes', *Lord Berners (1883–1950)*: The Triumph of Neptune; Nicholas Nickleby – Incidental Music from the Film; Trois morceaux; Fantaisie espagnole. Teldec Records, EL 27 05011 (1986). Reissued on CD: EMI Classics CDM 5 65098 2
Hurd, Michael	'CD Liner Notes', *Lord Berners (1883–1950)* (Lord Berners: Songs, Piano Music: Marco Polo 8.225159, recorded 1998, issued 2000)
Lane, Philip	'Sleeve Notes', *English Piano Music Four hands* (Auracle Records AUC 1001, 1981)
Lane, Philip	'CD Liner Notes', *Lord Berners (1883–1955)* (The Triumph of Neptune; L'Uomo dai baffi; Valses

	bourgeoises; Polka: Marco Polo 8.223711, recorded 1996, issued 1998)
Lane, Philip	'CD Liner Notes', *Lord Berners: Complete Vocal and Solo Piano Music* (Lord Berners: The Complete Vocal and Solo Piano Works, Albany Records, TROY 290, recorded 1994, 1996, issued 1997)
Lane, Philip	'CD Liner Notes', *Lord Berners (1883–1955)* (Wedding Bouquet, Luna Park, March: Marco Polo, 8.223716, recorded 1994, issued 1996)
Lane, Philip	'CD Liner Notes', *Lord Berners (1883–1955)* (Ballet Music: Les Sirènes, Cupid and Psyche, Caprice Péruvien: Marco Polo 8.223780, recorded 1994, 1995, issued 1995)

Catalogues, Music Dictionaries and Encyclopaedias

BBC	*BBC Music Library Piano and Organ Catalogue Volume 1* (London, BBC, 1965) Piano solos 7, Piano duets 84
BBC	*BBC Music Library Song Catalogue Volume 1* (London, BBC, 1966, 110)
Compton, Sheila	*BBC Music Library Orchestral Catalogue Volume 1* (London, BBC, 1982)
Farish, Margaret K	*Orchestral Music in Print* (Philadelphia, Musicdata Inc., 1979)
Slonimsky, Nicolas	*Baker's Bibliographical Dictionary of Musicians* (New York, Schirmer Books, 8th edition, 1992, 172)
Thompson, Oscar (ed.)	*The International Cyclopedia of Music and Musicians* (J M Dent & Sons Ltd, London. First pubd USA 1938, England 1942. Revised edition ed. 1956)

****

In addition, a file of correspondence between Berners and the BBC, 1935–1944, is kept at the BBC Written Archives Centre, Reading.

Berners was BBC Radio 3's 'Composer of the Week' 17–21 April 2000. Donald McLeod presented five hour-long programmes dedicated to his music.

Index